BEYOND THE
SAND AND SEA

BEYOND THE SAND AND SEA

*One Family's Quest
for a Country to Call Home*

Ty McCormick

St. Martin's Press

New York

First published in the United States by
St. Martin's Press, an imprint of St. Martin's Publishing Group

www.stmartins.com

Library of Congress Cataloging-in-Publication Data

Names: McCormick, Ty, author.
Title: Beyond the sand and sea : one family's quest for a country to call
  home / Ty McCormick.
Description: First edition. | New York : St. Martin's Press, 2021.
Identifiers: LCCN 2020047433 | ISBN 9781250240606 (hardcover) |
  ISBN 9781250240613 (ebook)
Subjects: LCSH: Hussein, Asad, 1995– | Dadaab Refugee Camp. |
  Refugees—Somalia—Biography. | Refugees—Kenya—Biography. |
  Refugees—United States—Biography. | Somalis—Kenya—
  Biography. | Somalis—United States—Biography. | Refugee
  camps—Kenya. | Somali-Ethiopian Conflict, 1979– | United States—
  Emigration and immigration—Government policy.
Classification: LCC HV640.5.S8 M335 2021 | DDC 362.87096773—dc23
LC record available at https://lccn.loc.gov/2020047433

Our books may be purchased in bulk for promotional,
educational, or business use. Please contact your local bookseller or
the Macmillan Corporate and Premium Sales Department at
1-800-221-7945, extension 5442, or by email at
MacmillanSpecialMarkets@macmillan.com.

First Edition: 2021

10 9 8 7 6 5 4 3 2 1

For Oma and Grandmother,
who taught me how lucky we are to live in a country at peace

Contents

Introduction   1

Book One: Origins

I.   Desert Macondo   17

II. A Sister's Love   39

III. The Torture Chamber   62

IV. Tahrib   81

V.   Striking Out   93

VI. Help from Afar   107

Book Two: Journeys

VII. In the Footsteps of Al-Shabab   129

VIII. A Beacon of Hope   150

CONTENTS

IX. Culture Shock   164

X. Miracle   179

Book Three: Reflections

XI. America at Last   209

XII. Princeton   226

XIII. Goobe   239

XIV. A Sense of Belonging   264

Author's Note   *271*

Acknowledgments   *275*

About the Author   *279*

Introduction

New York, July 2017

As he stood in line for immigration at John F. Kennedy International Airport, Asad Hussein tried to recall the final stanza of a poem by William Ernest Henley. In front of him, over the heads of a dozen disheveled travelers, stood a row of glass cubicles marking the border of the United States. Unremarkable as it must have seemed to the other travelers that day, the sterile, fluorescent-lit gateway to America felt surreal to him. Years before, in a desert refugee camp in East Africa, he had scrawled the poem on a slab of sheet metal he used to keep the sand from blowing into his tent. Henley's words had famously sustained Nelson Mandela during his long imprisonment on Robben Island, and Asad had sought in them a similar source of inspiration. He had hoped they would strengthen his resolve to one day reach the United States.

It matters not how strait the gate,
How charged with punishments the scroll,
I am the master of my fate,
I am the captain of my soul.

How many times had he read those lines, growing up a citizen of nowhere in the world's largest refugee camp? A sea of sand and thorn scrub and makeshift tarpaulin dwellings in the dry badlands of northeast Kenya, the camp had been home to more than 500,000 people at one point—a city the size of Kansas City or Atlanta, except without electricity or running water. There were no paved roads, no two-story buildings, no permanent structures of any kind. Most of the refugees had fled the war in neighboring Somalia, but a growing number, like Asad, had been born in the camp and never seen their home country. Members of this new generation had spent their entire lives in limbo. Everything from food rations that kept them alive to the arcane resettlement process that offered the only hope of a better future hinged on the whimsy of distant powers.

In Dadaab refugee camp, no one is master of his fate.

Yet somehow, after twenty-two years of waiting, Asad had made it here. In his back pocket was a UN-issued travel document that contained a student visa. Tucked inside the document's light blue jacket was a form stating the impossible: He had been admitted to Princeton University and awarded a scholarship worth $70,000 a year. It was more than his entire family, perhaps his entire block in Dadaab, had ever seen in their lives, and so improbable that he hadn't allowed himself to fully process what it meant. He didn't dare. Too many times he had been on the cusp of breaking free from Dadaab only to have it re-ensnare him at the last moment.

There was the promise from the UN Refugee Agency of resettlement in the United States that had gone unfulfilled for thirteen years, the prestigious Canadian scholarship he had devoted his entire childhood to winning only to fall short of the grade, and the desperate attempt to smuggle himself out of the camp that had ended with him behind bars. Then came an executive order by President Donald Trump that shook Dadaab like an exploding mortar shell. Just days before his parents were scheduled for an interview at the U.S. Embassy in the Kenyan capital of Nairobi, the final step in the arduous vetting process for green cards, the United States suspended all refugee admissions and banned travelers from seven Muslim-majority countries, including Somalia.

Now as the customs line inched forward, he felt sure someone would snatch this opportunity from him as well. The Trump travel ban wasn't supposed to apply to him, since he had been born in Kenya and granted a student visa. But he knew the agents at the border had the final say on who entered the United States, and there were plenty of reasons they might turn away a twenty-two-year-old ethnic Somali man. Already, a mysterious American official had intercepted him on his layover in the Frankfurt airport. She had peppered him with questions, some of them surprisingly blunt: "Have you ever been a member of an extremist organization? Do you *know* anyone who is a member of an extremist organization?"

With each shuffle forward, Asad's anxiety grew. By the time he reached the front of the line and a young Latino agent with a crew cut beckoned with a pair of raised fingers, he could feel himself freezing up, the hint of a childhood stammer creeping back into his voice. *Just answer the questions the way you practiced,* he told himself. *Look the agent in the eye. Smile.*

The first few questions were pro forma: What did he plan to study? Was this his first time to the United States? The agent swiveled in his chair to face his computer screen. His sullen expression gave no hint as to what he was reading, but as the minutes dragged on Asad was overcome with a feeling of dread. Then, without warning, a light above him began to blink red. "Would you come this way, please?" the agent said, stepping out from behind his desk and gesturing to a dimly lit hallway at the end of the row of cubicles. "We'd just like to ask you a few more questions."

...

I first met Asad about a year and a half earlier, a day or two after Trump announced his travel ban. At the time, I was the Africa editor of *Foreign Policy,* a small American magazine owned by the former Washington Post Company. My job was to rove the continent in search of stories, and to commission articles from other correspondents whenever news broke and I couldn't cover it myself. I had recently visited Dadaab to write about Kenya's threats to close the camp and expel its hundreds of thousands of inhabitants. I had also read an article in the *New York Times Magazine* by a young man who had grown up in Dadaab. Detailed and emotionally wrenching, it told the story of his sister's first trip home to the camp after eleven years in the United States. Because it was so well written, I assumed the author had been one of the lucky few to receive a scholarship to study abroad. It didn't occur to me that he might still be stranded in the camp. When Trump announced the travel ban, I reached out to the young man on Twitter to see if he would be willing to write something about families that were affected, not thinking that his would be one of those families. "This is such sad news for me personally," Asad replied. "It somehow seems the world is working against us."

It was only after he agreed to write the article and we met in person to discuss it that I discovered he had never been to college. He had traveled to Nairobi expecting to see his parents off to America, so we met on the ground floor of a gleaming, modern shopping center at a café popular with the Somali diaspora. Over steaming lattes near a glass elevator bank mobbed by hurried shoppers, he told me about his childhood in the camp, where there are no elevators, no lattes, and nowhere to rush to or from. He told me about how the resettlement process had disrupted his education multiple times, and about how for years he had sneaked into the library at night to teach himself what he had missed in the classroom. He read Tolstoy, Dickens, and García Márquez, designing a kind of "Great Books" education for himself from the dog-eared volumes donated by American charities. Whenever he encountered a word he didn't know, he looked it up in a battered copy of the Oxford English Dictionary.

Asad is tall and lanky and wears thick, rectangular glasses that accentuate his already bookish appearance. He can be wildly animated, swinging his arms like a conductor as he rails against injustice or expounds on what he sees as the absurdities of life outside Dadaab. In between vignettes from his childhood, he peppered me with questions about my life. I sensed that he was mining me for information about the world beyond Kenya—a country that he had still never left. I had been to Somalia the previous year and embedded with African Union troops fighting al-Qaeda-linked militants not far from where Asad's father was born. Asad had read my articles, and he wanted to know more about how it looked and felt and smelled. "How did you find it?" he asked me. "You know, I have never been to my own country. It's crazy."

Despite his frustration at having been denied access to so many things others took for granted, he seemed genuinely grateful for what he had gotten in the camp. "I was so privileged," he said more than once. "To be in a place where there were aid agencies, it was a great privilege. In those days, the schools in Dadaab were outperforming the schools in the rest of northeast Kenya. We had a beautiful library built by an NGO—it's not there anymore, people took the books—but back then we had a beautiful library. I had the whole world at my fingertips."

The first residents of Dadaab arrived in 1992, a year after Somalia collapsed into civil war and more than a decade before mobile phones came widely into use. A quarter of a century on, residents can peer out at the rest of the world through Facebook and Twitter, but they remain trapped in an environment that is virtually unchanged, save for the steady creep of the desert into the semi-arid shrublands that once yielded firewood and game. The tents still buckle against the windblown sand, still get swept away by periodic floods. Their occupants now include second- and third-generation refugees—permanent exiles facing a lifetime in waiting.

Kept alive but prevented from living, the residents of Dadaab have clung to one eternal source of hope: resettlement overseas, sometimes in Europe or Canada but mainly in America. Since the end of World War II, when it opened its borders to more than 650,000 displaced Europeans, the United States has taken in more refugees than the rest of the world combined. In the last three decades alone, it has accepted nearly three-quarters of the more than 4 million refugees resettled anywhere in the world—more than Canada, Australia, Britain, and thirty-three other designated resettlement countries added together. That number represents only a tiny fraction of the total in need of asylum—the vast majority of refugees will never be resettled—but for a time it transformed the United States into a beacon of hope for millions of people around the globe. In Dadaab when Asad was growing up, nearly every aspect of life revolved around getting to America. For the tens of thousands of people who were in the U.S. resettlement pipeline at any given moment, America was the subtext of every conversation about the future, of every promise that someday things would get better.

Perhaps nowhere else on earth have so many people placed so much faith in a country they have never visited and are unlikely ever to reach. And perhaps nowhere else on earth have the results of a distant presidential election proved so utterly devastating. When Trump announced his travel ban in January 2017, there were more than 14,000 refugees at some stage of the resettlement vetting process in Dadaab. Some, like Asad's parents, had waited decades for an interview. Others had received their visas only to have their flights canceled at the last moment.

The bar on refugee admissions was eventually lifted, but the resettlement pipeline from the countries affected by the travel ban remains mostly blocked. Just eight refugees from Dadaab were resettled to the United States in 2018 and fourteen were resettled in 2019. Even those with life-threatening illnesses have been denied travel authorization to seek medical care in the United States. Some of them have died. Yet that January afternoon in 2017, it was clear that Asad hadn't lost faith.

The story of his escape from Dadaab, and of his improbable leap into the Ivy League, is a marvel of endurance and fortitude, Henley's famous evocation recast for the modern age. It is also a chronicle of happenstance, of long odds and impossibly good luck, and of uncommon generosity. At various times, I feared it might turn out very differently. In that regard, it is also the story of the Asads who might have been—of his younger sister who died of malnutrition and is buried in a sandy unmarked grave, of his older sister who dropped out of school in the sixth grade but somehow managed to carry the rest of the family on her shoulders, of his brother who lost hope and spends his days chewing a stimulant leaf known as *miraa*.

So many futures were far more likely than making it to a university of any kind: recruitment into an extremist group, a dangerous sea crossing in search of work, death at the hands of Kenyan security forces who have killed and disappeared thousands of young Somalis. These were paths followed by many of Asad's classmates and friends. He is the only person born in Dadaab ever to be admitted to Princeton University.

. . .

From the baggage-claim area behind immigration control, I watched helplessly as the agent led Asad away. I had already collected his luggage and mine, and was pacing anxiously in front of an empty carousel. For the past eighteen months, we had spoken almost every day. After our initial meeting in the mall, he had written another moving essay that chronicled his lifelong fascination with the United States, a place, he wrote, that "other refugees spoke about the same way they spoke about the hereafter." Like so many of the immigrant writers he admired, from Junot Díaz to Vladimir Nabokov, he hoped to find his voice writing novels in America—if only he could ever make it there. "The words I write may travel all around the world, but I am confined to the refugee camp where I was born," he wrote. "I can't move freely in Kenya; I need a permit to leave Dadaab. My whole life, it seems, I've been living the American dream. I just don't know how much longer I can bear to live it outside of America."

We kept in touch after his essay ran, exchanging articles and tidbits of news about Dadaab. When he decided to remain illegally in Nairobi and apply to a prestigious boarding school, my wife and I agreed to pay the one-third of his tuition that wasn't covered by a scholarship. By then Asad and I were meeting regularly at a crowded outdoor café set off from one of Nairobi's busier roundabouts. Our informal interviews lasted hours, and often drifted into discussions about writing, journalism, and ethics. We bantered back and forth about the line between journalistic inquiry and political activism. It was important to

Asad for journalism to serve a moral purpose. At one point, he sent me a *New York Times* article about a reporter whose life had become deeply intertwined with that of her subject, a terminally ill cancer patient. It was the kind of reporter-subject relationship journalism professors warn their students against, but in this case, it had resulted in a beautifully honest story.

It occurred to me that our lives were also becoming intertwined. The ethics of journalism demand a certain remove from our subjects. We are impartial observers, we tell ourselves, just here to witness and report back. But some stories test those artificial boundaries, and some shatter them altogether. The more of his story that Asad entrusted me with, the less I felt like an impartial observer. And the more time we spent together, the more outraged I grew at the obstacles he encountered that were mostly invisible to everyone else. In researching this book, I spent hundreds of hours listening to Asad recount memories from his past. But I also had a front-row seat to his present during a period in which his life's trajectory was altered so suddenly and dramatically that his own family couldn't fully comprehend what had occurred. That period was punctuated by near-daily setbacks and disappointments, however, as Asad attempted to break free from a universe defined by deprivation and into one of plenty.

There are so many ways in which the best universities in the world—nearly all of them located in rich countries—keep out people like Asad, people without bank accounts or credit cards, reliable access to the Internet or parents who can read and write. People who are de facto heads of households as teenagers and have younger siblings to clothe and feed. The application process was designed for residents of "a different world," as he put it, one where people had second homes to list on financial aid applications or "favorite keepsakes" to describe in personal essays. Even the most basic requirements had tripped him up. There was the online common application used by most U.S. universities that didn't have an option for stateless applicants, the teacher who refused to write a recommendation because Asad didn't have a full academic transcript from Dadaab, and the SAT examiner who turned him away at the door because of a scheduling mix-up after he had spent months preparing for the test.

When Asad finally emerged from the interrogation room at JFK and flashed me a thumbs-up, I felt tears well up in my eyes. It turned out that the mysterious official in Frankfurt had flagged him for additional questioning in New York, but Asad had managed to answer everything to the agent's satisfaction. The universe of plenty had thrown up one last obstacle, and as I had seen him do dozens of times before, he had found a way over. Still shaken and looking disoriented, he retrieved his luggage and we walked together into the humid summer sun. The ride into New York City took us through Queens and along a blighted stretch of Atlantic Avenue in Brooklyn, past desolate warehouses and crumbling brick tenements. A sign on one edifice advertised speedy eviction services. I wondered what must be going through Asad's mind after dreaming of this moment for so long. But for once, I didn't ask him and we drove on in silence.

Book One

ORIGINS

I

DESERT MACONDO

Luuq, Somalia–Dadaab, Kenya, 1991–92

Kaltuma had just given birth to her third child when the war arrived in her sleepy farming town, nestled in a bend in the muddy Jubba River. The smell of cordite wafted through the banana trees. The thud of artillery shifted the soil beneath her feet. Her husband Sharif said it was time to go. A former conscript in the Somali army, he knew the plague of death that was blowing their way. And so they gathered the children and started walking, leaving behind the sturdy mud-and-thatch home and the sprawling farm they had built together. It wasn't the first time war had intruded on their lives, but it was the first time they had a lot to lose: a stable, settled life, built on the seasons and the natural bounty of the land. Neither of them can remember how long they walked, the crackle of gunfire never far behind. Was it days? Weeks? The landscape went from green to brown. Clusters of fruit trees became spindly desert acacias. They carried only the essentials: clothes, food, a few shillings. The one keepsake they took with them was a box of handmade tools, relics from the colonial era that Sharif used to carve long wooden planks—*looxax,* in Somali—on which he inscribed Quranic verses.

In the waning days of his regime in the early 1990s, the Somali dictator Siad Barre is said to have vowed, "When I leave Somalia, I will leave behind buildings but no people." It was a prophetic quip from the man who presided over the near-total destruction of one of Africa's most promising democracies. In 1969, months before he seized power in a military coup, more than sixty political parties had contested a free parliamentary election. Mogadishu, the capital, was known as the "pearl" of the Indian Ocean. Two decades later, bullets had replaced ballots and the pearl lay smashed in ruins, its elegant seaside villas gutted and pocked with craters.

Overpowered by a coalition of rebel groups, Barre fled the capital in 1991 with what remained of his army. They took the country's foreign currency reserves with them, along with crates of gold bars and whatever else would fit in their convoy of tanks. In the quarter century of fighting that followed—first between rival warlords and then between Islamist militants and an intervening UN-backed force—somewhere between a third and a half of Somalia's population fled their homes.

Asad's parents and older siblings were among them. They

trekked on foot to neighboring Kenya, more than 100 miles along a dusty road littered with debris: clothing, pots, coils of foam bedding—objects grabbed in haste and later abandoned out of exhaustion. They passed the burned-out husks of vehicles, bodies decomposing in the sand. One day at dawn they were ambushed. Militants bore down on them in pickup trucks retrofitted with anti-aircraft guns. Chaos reigned for a few terrifying seconds as the vehicles careened to a halt, disgorging sinewy young fighters in tattered fatigues. But then the soft cry of a newborn rang out. Daahiro, Kaltuma's youngest, had awoken. The gunmen lowered their weapons, and their leader began shouting at Sharif, castigating him for taking his family through a region wracked by such heavy fighting. Then the militia leader ordered his men to give the family food, and urged them to hurry on before they were killed.

They arrived in Mandera sometime at the end of 1991. By then thousands of Somali exiles had poured into the remote Kenyan outpost that sits on the border with Somalia and Ethiopia. Their makeshift tents, rigged haphazardly from twigs and rags and faded UN tarps, spilled into the orange semi-desert in every direction. The international response to the Somali crisis was still kicking into gear, however, so there was little in the way of emergency assistance. A few harried doctors worked around the clock, but the sick and dying were too numerous for them to handle. Somalia was tipping into famine, and the emaciated figures streaming into Mandera offered an early preview of the suffering that would prompt President George H.W. Bush to launch a fateful humanitarian intervention the following year.

The journey to Kenya had been especially cruel to Daahiro. Ravaged by hunger, her tiny body had been reduced to a bird-like skeleton. A doctor diagnosed her with measles and severe acute malnutrition, an advanced stage of starvation in which the body essentially devours itself. Despite the doctor's efforts to save her with special high-calorie milk and other medicines, she died a few weeks later, and Sharif buried her in a shallow grave near the edge of the town.

Not long after Daahiro's death in early 1992, the UN began moving people to a new refugee camp it had opened 350 miles to the south. The conditions there weren't much better, but at least the refugees could register to receive regular food rations. The UN also promised improved medical care, which would enable Sharif to get treatment for cataracts that had clouded his vision in recent years. So the family packed their belongings once again and boarded a bus piled high with mattresses and plastic jerry cans. After a long journey on rough dirt roads, they arrived in Ifo, one of the three original camps that made up the Dadaab Refugee Complex. It consisted of hundreds of tiny plots laid out in orderly grids and enveloped by a permanent haze of dust. The land was flat as far as the eye could see. Aid workers directed them to Block A4, which they would later learn was prone to floods and crawling with scorpions.

A few weeks later, the aid workers returned looking for volunteers to plant trees. The camp was mostly devoid of vegetation, and the temperature regularly topped 110 degrees. A little shade would make it more bearable. But Kaltuma was convinced that the war in Somalia would end soon and they would all return home. She didn't plan on living in Block A4 for long, so she wasn't interested in planting trees.

...

Asad was born nearly four years later, in October 1995, although like many refugees born that year his birthday was officially recorded as January 1, 1996, for reasons of bureaucratic efficiency. His arrival coincided with the first in a series of misfortunes that would befall the family over the next two decades. After a complicated delivery, Kaltuma desperately needed a blood transfusion. But in those days, there was nowhere to get one in Dadaab. The nearest hospital with a blood bank was sixty miles away and inaccessible without a travel authorization from the government, something that could take weeks to procure.

Somehow, Kaltuma survived without a transfusion, but she remained bedridden for months. Her husband was incapacitated as well. Tall and bowed with a frizzy beard dyed red with henna, Sharif was in his early sixties and recovering slowly from his cataract surgery. It fell to his eldest daughter, Maryan, to keep the family going. After school, she worked in the market, selling paraffin, tea, and potatoes to supplement their monthly food rations. She bought the items from bulk traders and then resold them to passers-by at a slim markup, sometimes earning just a few shillings a day. She also protected her younger siblings from the bullies and petty thieves who preyed on children in the camp. Twelve years older than Asad and four years older than their brother Ibrahim, she was fierce enough to earn the nickname Askari, "soldier" in Swahili. Asad still wonders if he would have survived without her. Many did not in those days. Their graves were marked with little humps of sand that gradually melted away with time. When he was old enough to begin elementary school, the graveyard in Block A4 had disappeared entirely, covered by the tents of more recent arrivals from Somalia.

Those early years were the hardest. Often, they went to sleep with empty stomachs. But with so many people suffering around them, Asad and his siblings never thought to feel sorry for themselves. "You don't really understand what scarcity is, because everyone is living under the same conditions," he remembered.

Eventually, Kaltuma recovered. Four years later she gave birth to another son, Abdi Malik, and four years after that another daughter, named Habiba. Meanwhile, distant relatives arrived from Somalia and stayed with them until they could get settled elsewhere in the camp. Whatever there was to eat was divided by however many mouths there were to feed. That formula held even when the mouths belonged to orphans and other strays who arrived wordlessly at their home and sometimes stayed for years. People slept outside under the stars or near the hearth in the sand. When it rained, they all crammed under the single domed roof of the family's makeshift hut, fashioned from twigs and plastic scraps. They supported so many people that the neighbors began calling their mother by the nickname "United Nations."

As a child, Asad suffered from a stammer so severe that he could barely carry on a conversation. Embarrassed, he avoided playing with the other boys and rarely spoke in public. Neither of his parents had received any formal education aside from Quranic school, and Sharif's clan, the Ashraf, had been mostly shut out of Somalia's educational system before the war. In those early years, Asad can't remember any Ashraf children attending school in Dadaab aside from Maryan, whose precociousness extended to academic pursuits as well. Instead they worked odd jobs for Somalis from more powerful clans, reproducing the same hierarchies that had rendered their country unlivable. But Kaltuma had been raised in Ethiopia and was suspicious of clan politics. Some of her family had been educated, and she encouraged her son to go to school. "Convince your father. Tell him you want to go to school," she would tell Asad over and over.

But Sharif was skeptical. Though he was taciturn and aloof, he loved his children fiercely and could be overly protective. After Daahiro's death on the way to Kenya, he had never fully recovered. He worried that his son's stammer would expose him to ridicule in the classroom, a place he could not protect him. He was also hardheaded and disdainful of all forms of authority except for religion. The Ashraf clan's council of elders had voted to expel him years earlier, because he refused to abide by the decisions they made by consensus. "A man of his own head" was what they called him, and they didn't mean it as a compliment. Perhaps as a result of this rebellious streak, or perhaps because he recognized in his son an unusual budding curiosity, he eventually gave his assent for Asad to buck the Ashraf tradition and enroll at Abdul Aziz Primary.

In those days, the school consisted of two rows of squat rectangular classrooms, each of them framed with wooden beams and clad with old cans of cooking oil that had been hammered into flat sheets of metal. There were eight grades and only four classrooms, so the lower grades met outside in the schoolyard, in the mottled shade of the trees that Kaltuma had long ago refused to plant. "In two years there, I never did get inside a classroom," Asad recalled. Outside under the blazing equatorial sun, his classmates would nod off as the teacher read aloud from a textbook, reciting each lesson verbatim as if it were a religious text. Sometimes a gust of wind would tear loose someone's notebook, sending it tumbling across the dry, khaki-colored plain and the children careening behind it.

Asad was a clever student, but his father's fears were not unfounded. One day near the beginning of second grade, the teacher summoned him to the chalkboard and told him to write

"Monday." He spelled it "Munday," and then compounded his infraction by stammering as he tried to pronounce the word. His teacher, an older refugee named Halima who, like most of the teachers at Abdul Aziz Primary, had only an eighth-grade education, made him repeat it again and again as his classmates erupted with laughter. Soon tears were running down Asad's cheeks. Afterward she sent him home early with instructions to buy a special notebook for English class, a request she must have known would impose a significant hardship on the family. Like nearly all of his classmates, Asad took notes for all of his subjects in a single blue notebook provided by CARE International, a relief agency that administered most of the schools in Dadaab. Buying another notebook would require selling some of his family's food rations—and going hungry for a time.

When he arrived home later that day, he found his father sitting alone outside their hut. Sharif listened silently as Asad relayed Halima's directive. Then he shuffled wordlessly inside, emerging moments later with a twig roughly the size of a pencil. His eyes were red and his cheeks sparkled in the sunlight.

"Son," he said, his voice low. "You know, you can learn to spell in the dust." Then he began to carve the sand at their feet into the shape of letters.

"B-i-s-m-i-l-l-a-h," they read. "In the name of Allah."

. . .

The door to the clinic swung open and a chill breeze lashed Asad's face. Inside, rows of adults waited expectantly on plastic chairs as children milled about at their feet. Above them a strange white machine wheezed cold air into the room. Asad followed his parents and his older brother Ibrahim toward a row of empty seats at the back of the room, trailed by his two younger siblings and by Ayaan, a fourteen-year-old cousin who had been living with them for years. The whole family was nervous, but upbeat—it was good news that brought them to the medical clinic that day in 2004, when Asad was nine years old. They had just learned they would be resettled in the United States, because the UN Refugee Agency (UNHCR) had given priority to the Ashraf clan. It wasn't just educational disadvantages that the Ashraf faced; they faced increasingly hostile treatment from larger and more powerful clans. Ashraf families had been run out of their homes in Somalia; others had been brutalized or killed. As a result, it seemed, UNHCR was resettling practically everyone in Block A4 at once. Families were abandoning their tents and giving away all of their belongings. "Couples even stopped making love," Asad would write years later. "A pregnancy, it was said, could delay getting to America."

Swept away by the optimism, his parents had given away what little they had and promised their hut to another family. They had pulled Asad out of school, believing he would soon be in an American classroom where students had as many notebooks as they needed. Friends and neighbors had bid their goodbyes, boarding flights to American cities they had never heard of—places like Dearborn, Michigan, and Minneapolis, Minnesota, where tens of thousands of Somali refugees were being resettled.

Before Asad's family could join them, however, each of them needed to complete a medical examination. It was supposed to be a standard physical, with a TB test for anyone over fifteen and a list of required immunizations. But as they waited their turn in the chilly waiting room, Asad's parents knew something about the supposedly routine process that he did not, something that would end up haunting them for more than a decade as their resettlement case stalled.

The nurse in charge of the clinic at the International Organization for Migration, a UN agency that handled the medical examinations, was named Alibashir, but nobody called him that. Somalis are famously unsparing when it comes to nicknames. Someone who is losing his hair will inevitably be called Bidaar, or "Baldy," while an amputee can expect to be called Lugay, or "Legless." As cruel as they can be, these nicknames are usually bestowed as a sign of endearment. But that wasn't the case for Alibashir, who suffered from a degenerative spinal condition. He had acquired the nickname Goobe, "Humpy" in English, despite being universally reviled. He was notorious for his arrogance, and for mistreating the refugees under his care. Even before they arrived at his office, Sharif and Kaltuma had heard stories of his cruelty.

Goobe saw each patient individually in a private examination room. At the time, there were seven members of the family listed on the same resettlement case, No. 525765. It was Asad and Ibrahim, their parents and their two younger siblings, and Ayaan. (Maryan, who was married and over eighteen by then, had her own resettlement case.) The nurse called them in one at a time. When it was his turn, Asad heaved himself up onto the examination table, craning his neck to get a good look at the impressive row of medical instruments lining Goobe's desk. While another nurse slipped on a pair of latex gloves and rubbed a cotton swab over his shoulder, he asked Goobe whether his parents had passed their medical exams. Even at nine years old, Asad often translated for Sharif and Kaltuma, and he had come to think of himself as their guardian instead of the other way around.

Goobe didn't immediately look up from the file he was reading, and when he did it wasn't to respond. He fixed Asad with a disapproving look and then dismissed him with a wave of the hand. Asad wasn't sure what he had done wrong, but he was glad when the examination was over and he was allowed to return to the waiting room.

A few minutes later, the same nurse appeared and called Ayaan's name. She was the last to go in to see Goobe, and her examination lasted longer than the others' had. Slender and doe-eyed, Ayaan had recently begun to turn heads in Ifo. At fourteen, she was nearing the age when many girls were married in Dadaab, older even, than some of them. When she finally came out of Goobe's office after fifteen minutes or so, she seemed shaken and Asad wondered whether the nurse had been harsh with her as well. Many years later, he would learn what Ayaan had told his parents and sister: Goobe had asked her to marry him. When she refused, he had said, "You're not going anywhere."

. . .

After the appointment at Goobe's office, their family's resettlement case stalled. Six months later, they were told to report for medical examinations again. They were told the same thing six months after that and again after another six months. By then almost all of the Ashraf in Block A4 had left for America, along with the Somali Bantus, who had also been given priority on humanitarian grounds. The fifth or sixth time they repeated the medical examination, Asad overheard two nurses talking about his family. They were speaking in Swahili, as Kenyan aid workers often did when they didn't want the Somali-speaking refugees to understand them, and one of them asked why the same family kept coming back year after year. "Oh, it's so sad what Goobe has done to them," the other nurse replied.

Because she had gotten her own resettlement case when she got married, Maryan was unaffected by the troubles at Goobe's office. She and her husband received their travel documents in 2005, less than a year after their own medical examinations, and the UN whisked them away to begin new lives in Arizona. Maryan sent back gifts of clothing and money, most of which

Asad's mother gave away to those even poorer than them. One gift from Maryan that stayed in the family was a smartphone. It meant that Asad and his sister could keep in touch. She told him about the wonders that awaited in America, and he relayed a litany of disappointments from the camp. Their correspondence was intermittent, dependent on whether there was cell service and when there was money for phone credit. One rare bright spot to which Asad returned again and again was a library that had been set up at Ifo Secondary School after Maryan left. It had only a few bookshelves filled with donated titles, including a huge stack of *Reader's Digest* magazines, but to Asad it was a treasure trove. For Maryan, who had memories of Somalia before the war, stories had been an escape from the drudgery of refugee life. But for Asad they were a means of discovery, tantalizing pieces of a distant universe he hoped to one day explore.

After their parents pulled him out of school, he had begun sneaking in to the library at night to read. The night watchman, a man named Olat whose wife had known Kaltuma since they were children, would look the other way when he slipped in at dusk and out at dawn, bleary-eyed but feeling as if he was in possession of some cosmic secret. Sometimes Olat would let Asad take books home with him, and he would read them lying on his stomach in the sand, his face pressed so close to the kerosene lamp to compensate for his nearsightedness that his mother worried he would go blind.

The promise of resettlement still felt real then. And with his sister in America, he was overcome with the desire to learn about this distant land where anything was possible. He read American romance novels by Nicholas Sparks and Danielle Steel, and classics by Fitzgerald, Walker, and Salinger. He would often imitate the characters he read about. Holden Caulfield, the profane hero-narrator of *The Catcher in the Rye*, is forever encountering people and situations that strike him as "phony." The whole week after he read that book he was calling his friends "phonies" and saying "shit," "bitch," and "stupid," just like Holden. But he was especially interested in works by immigrant writers who came to America from impoverished and war-torn places, and who succeeded when they arrived. Chinua Achebe and Ngugi wa Thiong'o, but also Junot Díaz and Vladimir Nabokov. "I was going to be like them," Asad wrote later. "I dreamed of being a writer, and Maryan gave me hope. In America, she said, you can be anything you want."

By the time he was eleven or twelve, he had exhausted the contents of the library and was begging his sister to let him download e-books with her credit card on the family's shared phone. But he still had never traveled outside of Dadaab, which meant that much of what he read remained inaccessible. Cities, high-rises, and grand boulevards—Asad had seen none of these things when he first encountered them in books. They existed only in his imagination, constructed in his mind's eye from elements of what he knew. That made for some bizarre fantasies, he realized later. The first time he read *The Yacoubian Building*, by the Egyptian novelist Alaa Al-Aswany, he struggled to picture the setting. "It's about what happens inside an apartment building, but what is an apartment building?" he recalled. "How can you conceive of what lies entirely outside your realm of experience?" At the time, he imagined two flimsy huts like the one he lived in stacked on top of one another.

Unable to relate to much of what he read, he gravitated toward the magical and the absurd, things that should have been alien but instead felt oddly familiar in a place where so much was out of his control. Camus' *The Stranger* and Orwell's *Nineteen Eighty-Four* were frequent companions growing up, as was Paulo Coelho's *The Alchemist*. One day a friend brought him an English translation of *One Hundred Years of Solitude* by Gabriel García Márquez. The novel is set in Macondo, a town cut off from civilization by measureless swamps and forbidding mountain ranges. For many years, the only visitors are traveling gypsies, who arrive each spring to sell their wares, mainly technologies of dubious value like flasks and vials for alchemy. José Arcadio Buendía, the founding patriarch of Macondo, spends long hours in his study trying to unlock the hidden potential of each new technology. Eventually, he is driven mad. His final years are spent tethered to the base of a chestnut tree, muttering to himself in Latin.

Asad hadn't expected to recognize Macondo, or Buendía

for that matter. But like Macondo, the sprawl of tents he called home was severed from the rest of humanity, both by geography and by the invisible web of restrictions designed to keep him in limbo. Instead of gypsies, there were aid workers, who formed the only links to the outside world. The wares they peddled were more useful—the food and medical care they provided kept the refugees alive—but they were maddening in their own way. The schools in Dadaab often outperformed those in other parts of Kenya, but for the vast majority of graduates they served as conveyor belts to the same miserable future that awaited all of the camp's residents.

Asad read and reread the book, letting the florid prose roll off his tongue. It was delicious, he thought, lyrical and alliterative in a way that reminded him of the poems of his ancestors. Evocative language laced with repetitive mnemonic devices could be passed down orally from generation to generation. It could survive a mass exodus from Somalia in which so many other cultural artifacts perished. But what struck him most about *One Hundred Years of Solitude* was the profound way in which it seemed to articulate his own dilemma. Dadaab was a desert Macondo, he realized. He would either break free, or, like Buendía, he would die a madman under a tree.

• • •

Since he had stopped going to school, and since his sister had left for the United States, Asad had taken over most of the household duties. He rose early each morning and fetched water from the communal tap, waiting in line with dozens of women from Block A4 to fill his plastic jerry cans. Sometimes, they made fun of him for being the only boy at the pump. "You are not even supposed to be here," they would chide, often using his gender as a pretext to cut him in line. Mostly they just ignored him and complained about the men in their lives. Their husbands, it seemed, did little except gripe about the food they were served and waste the precious water that the women had stood in line for hours to procure. There were squabbles about status, who was first in line, and whether school-aged children should be allowed to fill their containers first so they could get to class on time. It was a kind of symposium of the dispossessed, Asad thought, a venue where common grievances were aired and communal tensions were defused. As always, he just watched and listened, a silent onlooker absorbing the finely calibrated social hierarchies on display.

Once he had made two trips to the water pump and hauled four heavy jerry cans home, he usually headed to the market in Ifo, a bustling commercial hub known as Bosnia. The precise origin of the name is in dispute, but it likely has to do with reports of the Balkan wars that dominated the radio waves around the time the market was established in the early 1990s. A jumble of rusty tin shacks that matched the faded russet hue of the desert, Bosnia was a place where small-time traders from the local community did business with Somalis, exchanging everything from sugar, tea, and livestock to black market contraband. Humanitarian rations traded on an informal secondary market, and truckloads of freshly cut *miraa* arrived daily, wrapped in banana leaves and sold by women in brightly colored headscarves. Asad's brother Ibrahim, who was eight years older than him and rarely around, liked to chew *miraa*, even though it stained his teeth and made his eyes rheumy. Asad would occasionally hear Ibrahim fighting with his parents, usually about money. Sometimes, Ibrahim would ask him for a few shillings, and Asad would always oblige. It was their secret.

Asad pushed his way through the tumult of Bosnia, stopping at familiar vendors to buy food for the evening meal: tomatoes, cooking oil, maybe a few scraps of meat. Most days he spent 100 Kenyan shillings, about one U.S. dollar, which came from Maryan and made his family better off than most. When the shopping was done, he would venture to the margins of the camp to collect brush or dried wood to use as firewood. Scorpions and snakes lurked among the brambles, as did predators of another kind. Stories abounded of women being raped while foraging for kindling. As a precaution, they often moved in groups, wrapping the twigs they gathered into tight bundles that they balanced precariously on their heads. Asad sometimes joined troops of neighbors and friends. Sometimes he foraged on his own.

Despite the ever-present dangers, his mind often wandered to the distant worlds he read about at night, to Macondo and other fantasylands. He still frequented the library, slipping out of the house after the last chores were done to browse for new books or return stacks of old ones. Each time, he would exchange pleasantries with Olat, the night watchman. Olat's daughter Bisharo was a few years older than Asad and the first person he had ever seen wearing a high school uniform. Few children made it past primary school in those days, so the memory stuck with him: a tall, confident girl in a blue shawl and white polyester headscarf that marked her as part of a rarefied club.

Olat was proud of his daughter's accomplishments, and he told anyone who would listen about the high marks she received and prizes she won, including a scholarship to attend university in a faraway place called Canada. Asad listened politely, but thought little of the old man's ramblings. Every time they met, though, Olat would ask if he was back in school yet. It had been close to four years since his parents had pulled him out, thinking they were headed to America. And although he didn't miss getting teased by the other boys or being lectured by Halima, he began to sense that he was missing out on something important. His old classmates were now in the sixth grade. It wouldn't be long before some of them graduated. When he broached the subject of returning to school with Kaltuma, though, she was adamant that he begin again where he had left off, rather than skipping ahead to rejoin his old classmates.

"She thought I was rigging the system," Asad recalled of his mother, who was a stickler for rules and could always tell when her children were trying to skirt them. She didn't mind if attending school meant he would be able to do less of the housework, but she wanted to make sure he wasn't getting special treatment. "She thought I was trying to catch up to those students without having the knowledge."

Soon after their conversation, Kaltuma accompanied him to school and spoke to the teacher herself, insisting that her son be given placement exams in math and English to determine which grade he should enter. It was only the second time either of his parents had ever visited school with him, the first being six years prior on his very first day of primary school. In the end, he performed well enough on both exams to skip ahead to the sixth grade, rejoining those of his classmates who hadn't dropped out or been resettled.

From then on, he arrived each morning early so he could arrange the rickety wooden desks and claim one in the front of the classroom, close enough to the chalkboard to make out the teacher's scribblings. At the end of the day, he was always the first one out the door when the bell rang, both because he had evening chores to do and because he knew the other boys liked to fight each other outside the heavy metal gate of the schoolyard. By the time they were slugging each other and rolling in the dust, he was halfway across the camp breaking firewood or waiting to fill his jerry cans with water.

Asad tried not to get too close to his classmates. Many of them still mocked his stammering and threatened to beat him up. But his easy mastery of the subjects inevitably endeared him to the more studious among them. He tutored some of his classmates in English—his fourth language after Maay (a southern Somali dialect spoken by his parents), Somali, and Swahili—and was rarely without his copy of *Common Mistakes in English*, a rumpled red volume containing 550 examples of typical errors. Grammar was one area in which he shared his mother's enthusiasm for rules, and as time passed he developed a well-earned reputation for nitpicking. One day, the teacher cheekily suggested he should be running the class instead of her. From then on, he was known as The Professor.

II

A SISTER'S LOVE

Tucson, Arizona, December 2010

Maryan cradled the phone in the small of her neck, clamping the receiver tight against her chin, and punched the sequence of numbers she hoped would reconnect her to the world she had left behind. The line crackled, then clicked over to Kenya's Telkom network. It had been hard to keep in touch with her family since she arrived in the United States. The $20 international calling cards she bought at 7-Eleven would run out of credit after five or ten minutes. Often, she couldn't get through at all because the line in Kenya was down. The separation weighed heavily on her. She felt alone and scared, trapped with a man she didn't love in a tight-knit community that had turned against her.

When she and her husband Yussuf had moved into the white

apartment complex on North Alvernon Way in Tucson, Arizona, just down the road from the Walmart and Fred Meyer, she assumed her parents and siblings would follow close behind. But it had been six years since then, and still no word on when the rest of her family would be resettled. Already they had missed so much of each other's lives: births, Ramadan celebrations, first days of school. Maryan had two new daughters, Ambia and Najma. She also had a new baby sister, Habiba, to whom Kaltuma had given birth after Maryan left. She had always wanted a little sister, ever since Daahiro had died on the way to Kenya. Now she had one, but they were separated by almost 9,000 miles. Meanwhile, Asad had sprouted into a lanky teenager in those six stolen years. The memory of him that she still carried in her head, of a quiet child of five or six drawing in the sand with a stick, no longer bore any resemblance to the gangly young man in the family photos he posted on Facebook.

Maryan had done everything she could think of to inquire about her family's resettlement case. She had spoken to representatives at the International Rescue Committee (IRC), the humanitarian nonprofit that helped her and her husband settle into their dimly lit one-bedroom that smelled of fresh paint. At first, the IRC staff had said they could see the case number in their system, and that it looked like it was progressing. But then after a year or two the case stopped showing up, as if it had been wiped from the database.

Maryan had also sent dozens of emails to Church World Services, the U.S. State Department contractor that vetted refugees in Dadaab for resettlement, as well as to the Joint Voluntary Agency, or JVA, which prepared the travel documents for those who had been approved. She knew she was unlikely to get an answer, but week after week she sent the emails, often when she was too overcome with grief to bother correcting her typos: "6 year ago my family got aproof . . . to came to usa my dad is old man and have to take tb medication and after 6 year there steel in the refugee comp," she wrote on December 18, 2010, a cool, cloudy day in Tucson. "I deserve some answers I think. [I hope someone] will take time to read my email and send me some info."

On the rare occasions that she reached her parents by phone, the case was all they talked about. They all believed Goobe had something to do with derailing it, but they had begun to wonder if he or another UN official had sold their place to a different family. Maryan knew of other people to whom that had happened. UN officials would approach a refugee family and say they could help resettle them for $2,000. Then they would swap the family's documents in for ones belonging to another family that had actually been cleared for resettlement. What had convinced Maryan that this had happened to her family was a text message she received out of the blue a year or two after she arrived in Arizona. The sender didn't reveal his identity, but he claimed to be able to remove the block on her family's case—for a fee. She had called the number, but the man on the other end seemed to lose his nerve, perhaps worried she was recording the call. She couldn't be sure, but she thought his voice sounded like Goobe's.

This time Maryan wasn't calling to talk about the family's resettlement case. She was calling to tell her parents something terrible, something she had been dreading for weeks and that she knew would devastate them. But after a brief silence, she heard a familiar automated voice on the other end of the line. *"Samahani, Mteja wa nambari uliyopiga hapatikani kwa sasa. Tafadhali jaribu tena baadaye,"* came the chirpy female voice in Kiswahili. Usually it made her heart sink, but today she breathed a short sigh of relief. "Sorry, the customer you are trying to reach is not currently available. Please try again later." The bad news would have to wait for another day.

. . .

Maryan was once her father's princess. She has only scattered memories from Somalia, of Sharif planting onions in the garden, of the harrowing trek to Kenya. Despite the constant hardships of a childhood mostly spent in Dadaab, she remembers being loved and doted on as a girl. "He was a superhero," she said of her father. Sharif and Kaltuma had lost everything in the war, but they managed to make their daughter feel as if she lacked for nothing. Sharif would bring her little gifts, and unlike the dads in the camp who regarded cooking as women's work, he sometimes splurged on meat and made stew when he wanted to cheer her up.

Maryan learned early on how to work the system, and if she wanted something, she would cry until she got it. Once, she saw a pair of shoes for sale in Bosnia. They were black with silver linings, and they cost 700 shillings, around $7. At the time, the family's only source of income besides food rations from UNHCR was 1,000 shillings that a distant relative sent each month. Spending 70 percent of the family's monthly disposable income on a new pair of shoes was clearly out of the question, but Maryan cried and cried for three straight days. Finally, Sharif carried her to Bosnia and bought her the shoes.

When he wasn't spoiling her, Sharif made sure Maryan studied the Quran. A devout Muslim who rose before dawn each morning to deliver the call to prayer, he was known around Ifo as Quran Akhriyoow, or the "Quran Reader." He drew a sharp distinction between religion and culture, and he hated when people he regarded as cultural zealots hijacked religion to suit their ends. "He didn't want me to be manipulated as a woman. He wanted me to know my rights," Maryan explained. "If you learn the Quran and the religion and your rights, then nobody can tell you what is right and what is wrong."

In addition to Quranic school, she attended Abdul Aziz Primary. She excelled at math and quickly soared to the top of her class. As the years wore on, she came to appreciate what her parents had sacrificed for her happiness. It wasn't just the gifts like the shoes, which she came to regret having badgered them for, but the feeling of warmth and safety they had given her in what she now recognized as a sea of despair. School, she realized, might offer her a chance to repay them. She wasn't sure exactly how, but from an early age she grasped that education held the key to a better future—not just for her, but for her entire family. "If I can solve for X," she remembered thinking in algebra class, "I can solve my life."

But by the time she was a teenager, school had become a place of fear. Early marriage was the norm in Dadaab. When girls hit the age of fourteen or fifteen, they began to face increasing pressure to get married and have children. Those who resisted could expect harassment and intimidation, as well as social ostracism—or worse. Maryan started having to fend off advances from older students and from teachers. She would be called to the principal's office under academic pretenses, only to be prodded and ogled. Some teachers made crude and suggestive remarks; others hinted she should marry them—or at least spend the night with them. "It was relentless. There was so much pressure at school," she remembered. "The value of a woman is just having kids, and staying home and looking after poor men. And that didn't work for me."

So Maryan dropped out before the end of the sixth grade. She had already been working to support the family, both during her mother's extended illness following the arrival

of Asad, and after Abdi Malik's birth four years later, which
meant yet another mouth to feed. She had hoped Ibrahim
would eventually share some of the responsibility, but by the
time he was twelve or thirteen he had drifted out of the family
orbit. He would disappear for weeks at a time, only to turn up
wide-eyed and disheveled, asking for money. Maryan knew it
was up to her to look after the family. If school wasn't the vehicle that would allow her to help them, work was going to be.

But even as the tea and potatoes she sold helped allevi-
ate some of their financial stress, she sensed a change come
over her father. Several suitors had come to ask Sharif for his
daughter's hand in marriage. At her request, he had turned
them all down. But there was a limit to his patience on this
matter. He might have believed that women had rights, but he
also believed their most important duties were as wives and
mothers, and he was getting tired of explaining why his daughter was shirking hers.

"You're not always going to be this young. You're going to
need kids to take care of you," he would tell her.

"I have Asad," she would always reply. "I don't need kids."

But Sharif was unconvinced, and Maryan knew she was
running out of time. Rather than defy him openly, which she
knew would tear the family apart, she decided to leave home.
Sharif had a son from a previous marriage who lived in Eastleigh, a heavily Somali neighborhood in Nairobi often referred
to as "Little Mogadishu." He agreed to take her in, at least until

she could find a job and survive on her own. So one day in 1999 or 2000, she doesn't remember exactly when, she bribed her way onto a UN truck headed for the capital. She knew it would be waved through the police checkpoints, allowing her to slip undetected out of the camp without a travel authorization.

After a brief stay with her half-brother, Maryan found a job cooking *mandazi* and *sambusa,* fried triangular pastries stuffed with spicy meat and lentils. The shop was cramped and hot, but it smelled of onions and *pili pili,* red chili peppers that made her nose tingle in a good way. She earned $60 a month, which enabled her to rent a tiny one-room flat. At the end of each month, she usually had $20 or $30 left over, which she would spend on clothes and food for her family. She would write Sharif's name on the package, as well as the destination: Ifo. Then she would give it to one of the bus drivers who plied the long, bumpy road to Dadaab. One or two days later, the package would arrive in Bosnia. The driver would pass it off to one of the errand boys who hung around the market, who in turn would find the Quran Reader.

Maryan liked the anonymity of city life. You could blend in there, and disappear in plain sight. You could also defy the gender roles that had felt like a straightjacket in Dadaab. A woman there couldn't earn "halal money," but in Nairobi, her money was as good as a man's—it was power, plain and simple, and having power felt good. There were still limits on what she could do, of course. Maryan told no one about her apartment, not even her employer, since living alone was taboo. But on the whole she felt unshackled, like a woman in the workforce was what she was meant to be. "I felt that I'm not just a little girl, that I'm not just a woman, that I'm not just a baby-making machine," she recalled. "Everything comes down to financial freedom."

But her family hadn't given up on marrying her off. She had another half-brother, Ali Hussein, who lived in Moyale, a remote frontier trading post that straddles the border between Kenya and Ethiopia. In late 2002, Ali's wife gave birth to twins and he asked Maryan to come help out around the house. Soon after she arrived, however, he began pressuring her to get married. At eighteen she was getting too old to be single, he said, and if she waited much longer people would think there was something wrong with her. More importantly, she lived in his house now, and he didn't want the neighbors whispering about her. He brokered introductions to three different eligible bachelors, but he wouldn't take no for an answer. They had several blowout fights before Maryan finally agreed to marry one of the men, an acquaintance of Ali's named Yussuf.

From the start, their relationship was troubled. A volatile, domineering man with brooding eyes and a stubbly salt-and-pepper goatee, Yussuf was fourteen years older than her and stubborn as a bull. He was from the same clan, the Ashraf, but he hadn't fled Somalia because of the war. Instead he had come to Moyale to do business, and he didn't know what it was like to be a refugee. He expected Maryan to wait on him like a servant, and to stay indoors and out of sight. She fought him at every turn, and their quarrels grew more fearsome by the day. "We came from completely different directions in life," she said. "There was nothing that connected us." Three months after they married, Yussuf moved out and vowed never to return. But Maryan was already pregnant, and it would be another ten years before she was finally rid of him.

. . .

A few weeks after Maryan gave birth to her first son, Mohamed, word came from Dadaab that her parents and younger siblings were going to America. The Ashraf had been given priority, and many from Block A4 were leaving at once. Believing her brief marriage to Yussuf had run its course, Maryan took the first bus back to Dadaab with little Mohamed in tow. She had yet to tell her parents about her husband, in part because there was part of her that always doubted their marriage would survive. Now there was no hiding the fact that she was married and a mother. Sharif and Kaltuma would never approve of her plan to leave without Yussuf. But if they were going to America, she was going too.

The sight of Maryan with an infant child was a shock to her parents. Her mother broke down in tears, and she and Sharif both begged her to reconcile with Yussuf. "Think of the damage you are doing to our reputation," they said. But Maryan was adamant that she was done with him. A day or two before the family was scheduled to begin the vetting process for resettlement, though, Yussuf showed up in Dadaab demanding to know why Maryan had left with their son. He had heard from family back in Moyale that the UN was taking her to America. Suddenly, the wife he had abandoned was his ticket to a better life.

Initially, Maryan rejected the idea out of hand. But her parents pushed and cajoled her. Divorce was simply out of the question as far as they were concerned. It wasn't just taboo; it was unspeakable, a religious and moral failing that she would take to the grave. Leaving Yussuf behind, she realized, would wound her parents in a way she could never repair. What's more, she harbored her own feelings of guilt at having agreed to marry him. *You picked this guy,* she thought. *You can't just walk away.*

Reluctantly, Maryan agreed to give her marriage a second chance. She and Yussuf hadn't had a legal wedding in Moyale, so they organized a hasty one at a mosque in Ifo in order to obtain the marriage certificate they would need to be resettled as a family. A sheikh named Jawad Abdi presided over the ceremony, and his signature is affixed to the bottom of a handwritten document from that day, specifying a dowry of "a cow of three years." Sharif's signature appears as a witness, above a statement clarifying that the improvised certificate, written in

English and in Arabic, "should serve as proof of said marriage because currently marriage certificates are out of stock."

Once they were officially wed, Maryan and Yussuf were given their own resettlement case with baby Mohamed, instead of remaining attached to Sharif, Kaltuma, and the rest of their children. That fateful decision, made to accommodate Yussuf, would end up splitting the family in two for years to come.

. . .

Maryan came off the plane in Phoenix carrying one-year-old Mohamed and a white plastic bag stamped with the blue insignia of the International Organization for Migration. In addition to immigration and work authorization papers, the bag contained a four-by-six-inch card bearing the lyrics to "The Star-Spangled Banner." Unlike the generation of Somalis that would follow her, including her three youngest siblings, Maryan hadn't grown up dreaming of the United States. The words "land of the free and home of the brave" held no meaning for her. All she knew was that she wanted a better life for herself and for her family. That meant being more than a mother and a wife, more than a woman for whom a suitable dowry was a cow of three years.

Their journey had lasted more than forty-eight hours, taking them from Nairobi to New York to Houston and finally on to Phoenix. Neither she nor her husband had ever seen an airplane up close, let alone ridden on one. Now as they exited the terminal at Sky Harbor Airport, Maryan suddenly froze in terror. In front of her was a glass-encased stairway that appeared to be collapsing. The steps were grooved and sturdy-looking, but they fell away, one after the other, each time she went to step on them. It took a moment for Maryan to grasp what was happening. The concourse had been relatively empty when they arrived at the top of the escalator, but now a small line had formed behind them and people were anxious to move.

"It's okay, you can walk on it," came the gentle voice of a woman behind her. The woman must have guessed they had just arrived from somewhere far away—Maryan in her black hijab looking fearful and confused, and Yussuf at a loss as well.

The escalator wasn't the only thing about their new life that seemed odd. When Maryan would ride the Number 11 bus with baby Mohamed, people would fawn over them and say what a cute daughter she had. It wasn't until she made friends with a few Americans that she figured out the source of the misunderstanding: children's clothes were gendered here, and Mohamed's light pink pajamas were throwing people off. The grocery store was another locus of confusion. For months after they arrived, Maryan kept buying things by mistake because the pictures on the labels were misleading. A packet of tea bags, for instance, showed huge cubes of sugar, which was what she had intended to buy. Nothing was packaged this way back in Kenya. You bought things loose, not in bags or plastic wrappers. But Maryan was curious and outgoing by nature, and she didn't mind learning by trial and error. In fact, she bought lots of things on impulse, without even trying to guess what they were. A box of shiny red strawberries jumped out at her, so she bought them on a whim, only to recoil in disgust at what to her was their strange, sour taste.

Many new arrivals in Tucson who had come from Dadaab, including Yussuf, had never lived outside of a small rural village. Some of the children had never seen the outside of a refugee camp. Maryan was unique in that she had lived alone in Nairobi. She also spoke decent English, and was used to a level of independence that was unusual in conservative Somali communities. This was a source of constant friction in her marriage, but it was also a font of opportunity in America. Because she could read and translate, she was an invaluable resource to the dozens of refugee families living in the area, the person inevitably called on to resolve all manner of misunderstandings with landlords, employers, and the police. It wasn't long before the International Rescue Committee started hiring her for little jobs assisting other new arrivals, translating at job interviews or helping decipher training videos. She liked helping other refugees, and she could make as much as $75 for a single day of work.

With the help of the International Rescue Committee, Maryan soon got a full-time job at Jack in the Box, cutting tomatoes and iceberg lettuce for Caesar salads. The pay was only

$5 per hour, but the work was more regular than the translating jobs and the restaurant was close enough to the apartment complex that she didn't have to waste money riding the bus. There were a few mishaps in the beginning, like the time she called a colleague fat and caused her to break down in tears. In Somali culture, girth signifies wealth, so she hadn't anticipated this reaction. But on the whole, things went smoothly on the food-prep line. She made friends with her manager, a young woman named Nancy Rodriguez who was also a new mother in a tempestuous relationship. The two women liked to gossip and often confided in each other when things weren't going well at home. Sometimes, Nancy would knock quietly on Maryan's window at 3 a.m. or 4 a.m. Maryan would slip out of the house, careful not to wake Yussuf, and zoom off with Nancy in her silver Honda Civic. The two of them would drive for hours before the sun came up, talking and listening to music. Eventually, Nancy started letting Maryan drive, teaching her to maneuver along quiet back roads even though she didn't have a license.

Yussuf was having a different experience in his new country. Much less comfortable than his wife in their new surroundings, he was even more determined to control her than he had been in Kenya. The International Rescue Committee had helped him get a job, too, first as a night-shift cleaner at the Hilton and later as a landscaper. But the work was hard and he was constantly confused and embarrassed. Unable to speak

English and unwilling to learn, he took his frustrations out on Maryan. He disliked that she worked, and he hated that she thought it earned her a measure of autonomy. The way Maryan saw it, she brought in more than half of their income, so she should have at least half the say in how the household was run. Yussuf disagreed, often forcefully. Over time, their fights grew even more ferocious. She would yell and cry, and he would slam his fists against the tables and the walls. Sometimes, he would physically block her from storming out into the hall. More than once, the neighbors called the police. But there was part of Maryan that felt sorry for Yussuf, part of her that knew she couldn't leave him in a place where he couldn't survive on his own. Each time the cops came, she kept her mouth shut.

Yussuf seemed threatened by Maryan's prominent position in the community. He grew incensed when people he didn't know called the house asking for her, and several times he ripped the phone out of the wall. He also tried to sabotage Maryan's friendships by spreading rumors that she had neglected their son. Once, when he and Maryan were meeting with an employment counselor at the International Rescue Committee, he announced that he had forbidden her from working outside the home. The counselor calmly reached across the desk and lifted up baby Mohamed, who had been swaddled in Maryan's arms, handed him to Yussuf, and told him to take the bus home. "You can control your child," she

said flatly, "but in America, you can't control your wife." En-
raged, Yussuf stormed out of the room with the baby, a torrent
of insults pouring out of his mouth in Somali. "You just follow
the *cadaan*," he sneered at Maryan, using the Somali word for
whites. "You just follow their rules, and you don't respect our
religion."

. . .

Maryan began to dread being in the apartment. Whenever
Yussuf was there, she would find an excuse to go somewhere
else with the baby, whether it was to the Reid Park Zoo with
Nancy, who had a yearlong entry pass, or to Chuck E. Cheese
with other friends from work. But the bond between her and
Yussuf wasn't completely severed, and feeling lonely and iso-
lated, she sometimes let herself be drawn back into his arms. A
little more than a year after they arrived in Arizona, she realized she was pregnant again.

Ambia was born with jaundice, a common blood disorder
that made her skin appear slightly yellow. "You have a cursed
child," Yussuf said, when he first laid eyes on her at the University of Arizona Medical Center. The doctors said she would
be just fine, but that Ambia needed to stay overnight for special therapy under a halogen light. They discharged Maryan,
though, and told her to go home with Yussuf, a notion that
struck her as preposterous. She wasn't about to leave her baby
in the care of people she didn't know to be treated with a light

machine she didn't trust. In Kenya, no mother would leave her newborn at the hospital, but here the impassive white-robed physicians clearly expected her to. She broke down crying, and implored them to let her stay. Eventually, they relented, and Maryan and Ambia were given a room together for the next three nights.

A few weeks later, when they were back home at the apartment on North Alvernon Way, a bill arrived in the mail. When Maryan read it, she let out a gasp: $16,000, for the care she and her daughter had received. It was more than a year's salary at Jack in the Box. A knot forming in her chest, she dialed the billing department, unsure of what exactly she would say. But after she gave her patient code and verified her date of birth, the woman on the other end of the phone sounded surprised Maryan had called. "I'm showing no balance owed," she said. "It's been paid in full."

Maryan never found out who paid that bill. She wondered if maybe it was the employment counselor from the International Rescue Committee, a woman whose name she can't recall but who was always kind to her. Two years later, after her second daughter, Najma, was born, Maryan got up the courage to ask the counselor if she had been the guardian angel who had wiped out her debt. The woman scoffed at the suggestion. "I don't have that kind of money," she said.

But the counselor did have ideas about how Maryan could earn more money of her own: by pursuing a GED. With a high school equivalency certificate, a whole range of new job opportunities would open up—ones that paid better than $5 per hour and wouldn't leave her clothes smelling like fried food.

Soon, Maryan was spending several hours a day at Pima Community College while an elderly Somali woman in their apartment building looked after the children. Maryan liked being back in school, but in the beginning, she was bewildered by her classmates. They put their feet on their desks and ate food during class. Acting like that at Abdul Aziz Primary would have earned you a beating. Were these students not afraid of the teachers? Did the teachers have no self-respect?

One of her courses at Pima was English as a Second Language, or ESL. Most of the assignments were simple worksheets that involved identifying errors in grammar or spelling. But the worksheets were supposed to serve a secondary function as well: introducing foreigners to American traditions and customs. Tailgating at sporting events was the subject of one memorable ESL worksheet, which advised students that the boozy tradition was "a fun part of college life and for sports fans in Illinois." Maryan often found herself giggling quietly over assignments like these, which struck her as random to the point of absurdity. They weren't even *in* Illinois, she thought to herself. And why on earth would she ever need to know about drunken college football parties?

Six months later, Maryan had her GED. Not long after that she got a job at St. Joseph's Hospital, mopping up the surgical theater after operations. The pay was better than at Jack in the Box, and she was able to afford a drivers' education course and eventually a used car. She was also able to send more money home to her parents. There had been all manner of expenses to cover, including tuberculosis medication for her father, whose health had taken a turn for the worse. Lately, she had also noticed additional charges on her credit card statement for e-books that Asad had downloaded. The books were expensive, certainly more money than she would have spent on small luxuries for herself. But remembering the monotony of life in Dadaab, she was glad her brother was passionate about something. She hated to think of him whiling away his days in the heat, waiting in humiliating food distribution lines, and cooking over a fire pit. Books seemed to light him up, and thinking of him that way made her happy.

The two of them corresponded more frequently as the years wore on and Asad matured into a reserved and sensitive young man. She would create email and social media accounts for him so they could communicate more easily, then give him the log-in credentials over the phone. Sometimes, she would get email alerts warning that someone was trying to access her accounts from abroad. Those emails always made her smile.

She had come to think of Asad not just as a little sibling in need of direction, but as a partner in caring for their parents— she as the breadwinner in Arizona and he as the caregiver and problem-solver at home. Now instead of talking to Sharif about difficulties with doctors or the UN, it was always Asad she coordinated with. His was a comforting voice on the other end of the phone, and as time passed she felt herself leaning on him as well. When he was young, she had tried not to burden him with her own struggles. But the worse things got with Yussuf, the less of her suffering she was able to hide. It was strange opening up to someone she remembered only as a small child, someone whom fate had taken away from her and whose life was now so different from hers. They existed in totally separate universes, and yet there were things that only he could understand.

· · ·

Maryan had another phone besides the one she used to call home with her $20 calling cards. It was slim and black and its existence was a closely guarded secret. In the contacts, there was only a single number saved: 911.

The emergency phone had come from a domestic violence counselor. Because Maryan had high blood pressure and crippling anxiety, her doctor had come to suspect she was in danger at home and referred her to a shelter for battered women. Even before that Maryan had thought about running away with her children, but she didn't know whom she could trust or where to turn for help. Yussuf had succeeded in turning much of the refugee community against her, spreading vicious rumors about his wayward "Western" wife who thought she was better than other Somalis and didn't value their traditions. Even the idea of domestic violence was viewed with suspicion by many of the refugees she had helped translate for over the years. "If you are married and your husband beats you up, you have nothing to say because he's your husband," was how she summed up their thinking.

Yussuf never hit Maryan, but his constant emotional and psychological abuse had slowly broken her down. She would wake up in the middle of the night, heart racing, unable to bear the thought of another day with him. Even so, she felt paralyzed. Faith had always been important to her, and while divorce was technically allowed in Islam, it would make her an outcast. There was part of her that felt she had a religious duty to stay in the marriage as long as her husband did. And nothing had changed her belief that leaving Yussuf would crush her parents and forever change the way they looked at her. Running away to avoid getting married had been one thing. Divorcing the father of her three children would be quite another. "It felt like there was something holding me down that was heavier than me," she recalled. "Like I was in the ocean and the waves were just overpowering me."

But the situation had become untenable. She had started breaking down in public, crying in front of coworkers and in the middle of shifts at the hospital. She had missed work after one particularly painful fight, and then she had missed another day and another. Eventually, her boss had let her go. Yussuf had finally gotten his wish: a wife without a job.

Not long after that Maryan found herself alone on a ledge, looking down at what seemed like her only avenue of escape. As Yussuf pounded angrily on the locked door of their apartment, threatening to break it down, she teetered on the edge of a sliding-glass window, the smooth pavement of the parking lot beckoning from twenty feet below. She had reached the limit of what she could take. But as she contemplated stepping out of her life, it occurred to her that Yussuf probably wouldn't care if she died. The thought of his indifference filled her with rage, and she pulled back from the ledge. Suddenly, she knew what she would do, and it was something that would hurt Yussuf, too. The next day, she sold her car and bought four plane tickets to the farthest place from Arizona she could think of that was still in the United States. Then she picked up the phone to tell her parents she was leaving Yussuf and moving the kids to Seattle.

III

THE TORTURE CHAMBER

Dadaab Refugee Camp, Kenya, December 2010

The world came to Asad in Ifo, but slowly and in scarcely comprehensive snippets. Newspapers are still a rarity in Dadaab, but he remembers the first time he got his hands on one, at the butcher shop in Bosnia, where it was bundled around a slab of goat meat. Ice arrived a few years later, and he bought a big chunk just to watch it dissolve in a bowl of water. After ice came the Internet, bringing news and books and more frequent correspondence with Maryan. But by the time he graduated first in his class from primary school in late 2010, when he was fifteen years old, Asad had still never set foot outside of Dadaab.

That was about to change one bleary-eyed morning in December of that year, just as the first fires were being lit and the camp was stirring to life. With 800 shillings that Maryan had sent from the United States, the equivalent of around $8, he bought a bus ticket to Nairobi and took a seat next to the window. The lumbering oversize buses rumbled out of Bosnia each day at dawn and into the capital city one or two days later, depending on traffic. They were one of the few reliable lifelines to the rest of Kenya and to the world beyond, albeit one that was only accessible to Kenyan citizens or to refugees with the proper documents.

The national ID, *kitambulisho* in Swahili, is the passport that enables freedom of movement in Kenya. During the British colonial era, it was worn around the neck in a heavy metal box called a *kipande*, to be furnished on command in accordance with the Native Registration Ordinance. Now it looks like a driver's license, a laminated card bearing a photograph and fingerprints. And although it no longer serves as a tool of imperial domination, its absence can still elicit violence from the state. Refugees aren't entitled to national IDs, and temporary workarounds like "alien" cards and so-called "movement passes" are difficult and expensive to obtain.

Asad had no documents at all, and he knew little about where he was headed, save for the likely embellished stories he had heard about the capital city from the older boys at school. Nairobi beckoned like a forbidden fruit, a faraway universe full of riches and depravities so alien people spoke of them in whispers. Aside from stilted histories of modern Kenya, there were only a few books in the library at Ifo Secondary that were set in Nairobi. One was John Kiriamiti's 1984 thriller *My Life in Crime*. A fictionalized account of the author's long run as one of the city's most notorious bank robbers, it paints a lurid picture of Nairobi's criminal underworld in the years after independence—full of gangsters and prostitutes and trigger-happy cops. At one point, Kiriamiti—who goes by the alias Jack Zollo—evades arrest by shearing off his fingerprints with a razor blade.

In a way, the bus ride to Nairobi marked the beginning of Asad's life outside the law, if for no other reason than being a refugee in Kenya is to be effectively criminalized. The moment the bus rolled out of Dadaab and onto the dusty unpaved ribbon that runs sixty miles to Garissa, the first outpost on the long road to Nairobi, the authorities would regard him as a man on the run. This, in the retelling, is where Asad grows rather sheepish. He had no plan for avoiding the police on this first, fateful voyage outside the camp, and no money with which to bribe them to look the other way. "To be honest, it was a pretty bad idea," he said, adding that the only part of the journey he had planned in advance was to stay with a childhood friend who had moved to Eastleigh, the neighborhood in Nairobi where Maryan had gone when she left home years earlier. He hadn't told his parents where he was going or thought through what would happen if he were arrested. He had simply decided it was time to see what lay beyond Dadaab.

The bus lurched onto the main road. At first the landscape was familiar, the only one he'd ever known, full of coarse brambles and stubborn acacias whose flat tops looked as if they had been mowed. They passed camels and goats, stiff-legged men watching over their herds. Then the road emptied out. For miles, they bumped along without passing anything that hinted at human habitation. After about two and a half hours, the road turned to asphalt and suddenly they were gliding. Then just as abruptly, they wheezed to a stop. In front of them was a roadblock made from dented fifty-gallon drums. On either side were men in light blue uniforms. They were carrying guns.

The bus door swung open and the passengers filed off. Asad followed out onto the shoulder of the highway, where he joined the line of people waiting to have their documents checked. The process was slow and humiliating, as if it had been designed not just to extract bribes but also to remind the passengers of their lowly social status. The police made a show of ensuring that the photo on each passenger's *kitambulisho* matched his or her face. Then, using magnifying glasses, they compared the unique swirls on people's fingertips to the prints on their ID cards. It was a display of rigorous police work that might have impressed a younger Kiriamiti, but Asad was skeptical that the goal was anything other than to instill fear. "I don't even know whether that works or it's just bogus and scares people," he said of the fingerprint checks. In either case, he had no *kitambulisho* to hand over when he reached the front of the line, and his attempt to talk his way back onto the bus quickly failed.

The officers ushered him off to the side, where he joined several other unlucky travelers whose documents had raised suspicions. Soon, the bus was pulling away without them and he and the other detainees were piling into a green police truck with worn benches bolted to the side of an open flatbed. Unable to buy his freedom with money and unwilling to part with his only valuable possession, his phone, he was headed to the central police station in Garissa. The realization dawned on him gradually as the other captives pleaded with the officers, who kept increasing their demands as the vehicle approached its destination. It wasn't fear that settled over him, but indignation—righteous anger at being forced to participate in such a sham.

He had spent his entire childhood surrounded by exploitation, but his parents had gone to great lengths to instill in him a sense of right and wrong. His mother was selfless to a fault, and while his father could be headstrong and even harsh, Asad never doubted that the old man was guided by his own understanding of justice. Asad knew better than to expect the same from the authorities. After all, the bureaucracies that controlled so much of their lives—UNHCR and the other aid agencies—seemed largely indifferent to human suffering. Still, the crudeness of the corruption in this, his first real meeting with the Kenyan state, burned in a way that left him seething.

At the police station, the officers confiscated his belongings, including his shoes and belt, before shoving him into a crowded holding cell. The room was dark, except for a faint light that filtered in from a small window somewhere high above him—just enough so you could tell if it was day or night. The place was the size of a broom closet and it reeked of piss and shit. There were maybe forty prisoners crammed in there, all of them forced to stand shoulder to shoulder. People were pushing and shoving, using their elbows to gouge out space. He got knocked around at first, roughed up a little. But eventually some of the older prisoners took pity on him. "This is a kid," he remembered someone saying. "Give him space."

He spent the next three days in the crowded holding cell, taking turns with the other prisoners to lean against the wall, the only place it was possible to doze off for a few moments. The other prisoners were mostly Somalis, he discovered, and many of them had been there for weeks or months already. Some had come straight from Mogadishu, guided by human smugglers on the first leg of a longer journey through North Africa to Europe. But they had been intercepted by the police, and now the smugglers were ignoring their calls. They said they had spent thousands of dollars to get here—and for what? To be locked away in a stinking jail house? Asad had trouble explaining what he was in for. Nobody could understand why he hadn't given up his phone to avoid incarceration; the bribes the migrant Somalis were being asked for were much higher, far beyond what many of them would be able to pay. But a phone or a few thousand shillings for your freedom was a no-brainer in their view. "People start blaming you," he remembered. "They are like, 'Are you stupid?'"

Eventually, market forces prevailed, but only because Maryan intervened as she had so many times in the past. Using the informal *hawala* money transfer system favored by many Somalis, Maryan sent 10,000 shillings—or $100—enough to convince the guard to produce a rusty ring of keys and unlock the heavy metal gate. After returning Asad's possessions, the guard led him out to the street and told him to take the next bus back to Dadaab. "This is enough trouble for you, so just go back to the camp," he remembered the guard saying. But like his father before him, Asad was becoming a man of his own head.

. . .

Three days later Asad laid eyes on Nairobi for the first time. Instead of a bus back to Dadaab, he had found a truck headed to the capital and convinced the driver to let him ride along. The truck was old and overloaded with produce, unable to cover more than 100 or so miles in a day. They had stopped here and there at roadside villages, sleeping under the truck at night. The main highway into the city from the northeast, the Thika Highway, twists its way through a verdant landscape of coffee plantations and pineapple farms before climbing several hundred feet to Kenyatta University and the sprawling estates of Githurai and Kasarani. Concrete high-rises sprout up on either side, clustered so tightly that from a distance they look like a single impenetrable fortress. Most of the buildings are less than ten stories, with rough, unfinished exteriors and rusting metal roofs. But to Asad they seemed impossibly tall, like something out of a dream. The idea that humans were capable of building something that large—and that permanent—still didn't quite compute. "How the hell does this thing work?" he recalled thinking.

Eastleigh was even more astonishing. The streets were knotted with traffic, more vehicles than he'd ever seen: lorries and rickshaws and honking minibuses called *matatus* that belched black plumes of exhaust into the air. Throngs of people moved between them on foot, dodging motorbikes and stepping over potholes. Everywhere he looked, people were buying and selling things—clothes and electronics, spices and gold jewelry. It was like a thousand Bosnias, except in the shadow of block after block of towering shopping malls: AMCO Shopping Mall, Plaza Mall, Bangkok Shopping Mall, each one seemingly newer and more opulent than the last. Seeing it all for the first time was like discovering a "third eye."

Asad's friend worked during the day, so he wandered the city alone, gaping up at the high-rises. Several times he got lost and had to hail a motorcycle taxi because the buildings all looked the same to him—tall and shiny and like nothing that existed in Dadaab. Maryan had sent him some pocket money when he told her he wasn't going back home right away. He used some of it to buy the *Daily Nation* and was amazed to discover that it had been printed the same day. For years, he had been reading newspapers at the butcher shop in Bosnia, but by the time they arrived they were usually months out of date. He bought another paper the next day, and another the day after that, stacking them in a neat pile on the floor of his friend's apartment. Each day brought a new newspaper, populated by a totally new set of stories. Now that was pretty impressive.

The money Maryan had sent soon ran out. But before he began the long journey back to Dadaab, he stumbled upon a man selling used books on the street. On a whim, he bought a slim volume entitled *Half a Day and Other Stories*. It opens with a short allegory by Naguib Mahfouz in which a young boy goes to school in the morning and returns home in the afternoon an old man. The book was part of Kenya's national curriculum and years later it would be assigned to him for class. On that occasion, he would think back to his first trip to Nairobi, when it had felt as if he'd aged a lifetime in just a few days.

...

A few months before Asad decided to go back to school, the family had been forced to abandon their compound in Block A4. It had rained heavily for days on end, turning the vast bowl-like depression on the eastern side of Ifo into a fetid, stinking lake. They had hauled their mattresses, tarps, and other belongings through the flooded streets, past the water tap and the graveyard, to a new settlement in Block N9 that was on higher ground. Asad still remembers being chest deep in the blackened water, wading back to save his books.

By the time he graduated, the problem was too little rain instead of too much. From their new home, made from mud bricks hewn from the earth and dried in the sun, it was a twenty-minute walk to Bosnia along narrow sand paths flanked with prickly thorn scrub. Through the brambles, row after row of flimsy shelters seemed to multiply overnight. By the end of 2010, hundreds of new arrivals were streaming into Dadaab every day, mostly from drought-ravaged regions of southern Somalia. The annual *Gu* rains that typically revive the deadened landscape in March and April had failed in 2010 and were about to fail again in 2011, triggering the worst famine in sixty years. Roughly a quarter million Somalis would perish, and another 150,000 would be forced to seek refuge in Kenya, pushing the population of Dadaab over half a million and making it the largest refugee camp in the world.

Ever since he had seen Bisharo in her high school uniform, Asad had assumed he would one day follow her to Ifo Secondary School, then the only high school in Ifo. But as the population of the camp swelled and the classrooms grew overcrowded, aid agencies responded by setting up new schools. When the high school admission results were posted in early

2011, not long after he had returned from Nairobi, Asad was heartbroken to discover that he was bound for Towfiq Secondary School, a brand-new school that had fewer resources than Ifo Secondary and none of its history. At the time, only one in five teachers in Dadaab had had any formal professional training, and according to one charity's estimate, the ratio of students to textbooks was thirteen to one. The situation at Towfiq was slightly better, Asad discovered, but mainly because the vast majority of students had dropped out before high school, leaving more resources for the students who remained enrolled. Still, lack of basic supplies impeded instruction in nearly all of his courses. Whereas at Ifo Secondary there were beakers and rudimentary chemistry sets, students at Towfiq had to conduct imaginary experiments using the illustrations in their books.

Asad drifted aimlessly through the first few months of high school, resentful at having been denied a place at Ifo Secondary and questioning whether there was much to be gained from his new school. Even the novels he read in his spare time felt duller than usual, as if the cloud of disappointment that hovered over him had somehow enfeebled his imagination. But one day in April, Towfiq received an unexpected visitor who brought with him a much-needed source of inspiration. A stocky Kenyan in black trousers and a blue shirt that barely contained his girth, the man was a representative from the Windle Trust, an educational charity that ran many of the schools in Kenya. He addressed the entire student body from beneath a tree in the school yard, telling them about a potentially life-changing opportunity: a scholarship funded by the Canadian government that not only paid for university, but also allowed students to sponsor their families to come with them. WUSC, it was called, World University Service of Canada, and some fifteen to twenty of the top students in Dadaab won it every year.

Asad sat wide-eyed on a patch of dry grass, elbows on his knees, trying not to get his blue uniform dirty. This was the scholarship Bisharo had won, he thought, suddenly transported back to the library, where he had listened politely to her father on so many occasions. "This can be your way out," the man from the Windle Trust said.

This was Bisharo's way out, Asad thought. *Maybe it can be mine, too.*

. . .

Suddenly, a new route out of Dadaab had opened up, one that didn't depend on the decisions of distant bureaucrats or his willingness to risk imprisonment. It had been almost a decade since Maryan left for the United States, and still the rest of the family was trapped in resettlement limbo, awaiting final approval to join her. Lately, Asad had begun to doubt that they would ever be reunited. The scholarship held out the promise of a future he could control. Unlike the byzantine resettlement process, the requirements for the WUSC were simple and clearly articulated: score high enough on the national exam at the end of high school, and he would be eligible to apply. He felt invigorated, like his quest to escape Dadaab had taken an unexpected leap forward. For the first time in months, he felt the cloud lift and his usual sense of curiosity return.

One of the hardest things about being banished to Towfiq had been watching many of his closest friends go off to Ifo Secondary. Abdi and Muhiyadiin, who went by the nickname Bekar, or "Burger," because of his professed love of hamburgers (though no one knew for sure if he'd ever had one), had been part of informal study group with him for years. Abdi was tall and confident, full of jokes that made girls blush even when they tried to ignore him. Bekar, with his brooding eyes and narrow hairless chin, was stern but easily excitable, leaning heavily on the Swahili placeholder *nini* even when speaking English. Since they had gone their separate ways, Asad had hardly seen them. But the man from the Windle Trust had visited Ifo Secondary as well, and it wasn't long before Asad and his old friends were swapping notes about the future that awaited them in Canada and plotting a course to get there. They looked up older students who had won the scholarship on Facebook, and peered covetously into their digital lives. Here was the cousin of a neighbor, now studying engineering in Toronto, smiling with classmates in a wood-paneled auditorium. There was an older graduate of Ifo Secondary, dressed in crisp jeans and a soccer jersey, posing with a friend in a crowded sports arena. All of it contrasted starkly with the increasingly desperate situation in Dadaab as the famine raged in Somalia. All of it seemed to underscore the urgency of their new mission.

The three friends talked constantly about Canada. They didn't know much about the geography of the country, or which universities were located where, but Canada came alive in their minds. For Asad, it replaced America as the guiding light he could follow even in his darkest moments. It wasn't the famous melting pot that had absorbed so many of his literary heroes. But it was a land of opportunity he could reach all on his own, a place to which safe passage could be earned instead of bestowed.

To that end, Asad recommitted himself to his studies, signing up for the most challenging course load possible. Unlike other ambitious students angling for the WUSC, he didn't take Quranic studies, an easy A that would have boosted his GPA. Instead he doubled up on math and science, even though his real love was literature. He also resumed his impromptu study sessions with Bekar and Abdi, holing up in a vacant hut they christened "Room 101," or "The Torture Chamber," in a reference to Orwell's *Nineteen Eighty-Four*. The trio would camp out for long hours there, quizzing each other on isotopes or the structure of DNA. "We were very serious back then, serious beyond our years," Asad recalled. "You know, it wasn't like there were other options. It was the WUSC or it was nothing. You had to get this thing."

But there were lighthearted moments as well. The friends

devised a language of their own, with playful nicknames for one another and for the meals they enjoyed together. Each of them would swipe food from home to share during their marathon study sessions, parceling the spoils into separate courses they dubbed "Paper One," "Paper Two," and "Paper Three" in honor of the exam papers they were preparing to sit. Then they would divide up their actual subjects and take turns teaching each other. Asad was the humanities guy while Bekar taught math and Abdi took charge of chemistry and physics. Each of them tried to outdo the others by making their subject the most interesting. Sometimes they impersonated their teachers or adopted silly accents. Inevitably, Bekar and Abdi would get distracted and start talking about soccer, a topic that no amount of protestation from Asad could steer them away from. Bekar could drone on for hours about the game, and he had an uncanny ability to recall specific World Cup and Premier League games he had watched, something that delighted Abdi and irked Asad in equal measure. "Remember France versus Brazil, *nini*, 2002?" he would say. "Ronaldo scores two! Incrrredible!"

On the whole, these were happy days for all of them, days defined by frequent hardships but also by hope and companionship. Outside the sanctuary of Room 101, however, in drought-ravaged southern Somalia, a storm was slowly gathering force. Soon it would blow across the border into

Kenya, upending life in Dadaab and throwing their carefully laid plans into doubt.

...

The moment Asad realized things had changed forever came in the middle of chemistry class, one stifling hot day in November 2011. He sat near the front of the classroom as usual, absently thumbing the worn textbook on his desk and gazing at a plastic pull-down poster of the periodic table. His teacher, an exuberant young man named Ahmed, was chirping away about electrons and atomic orbitals. Suddenly, the classroom shook, and air rushed into his nose, ears, and mouth. A second later came the sound of an explosion, followed by shrieks in the distance. All around him the classroom erupted into chaos. Students raced for the door, upending desks and spilling stacks of papers onto the floor. Even before he arrived, blinking into the sunlight, Asad knew that something terrible had occurred.

Weeks before, on October 13, a group of gunmen thought to be from the extremist group al-Shabab, which then controlled much of southern and central Somalia, had kidnapped two Spanish aid workers from Dadaab. The two women had been working for the medical charity Médecins Sans Frontières, known in the English-speaking world as Doctors Without Borders, helping to build a new hospital in Ifo. Their driver had been shot, and the women spirited away to Somalia, where they would be held captive for the next twenty-one months.

Three days after the abductions, and partially as a response, Kenya invaded Somalia. It sent tanks and helicopter gunships across the border to create a buffer zone between the two countries, dubbing the operation Linda Nchi, Kiswahili for "Protect the Country." Inside Dadaab, aid agencies that had previously viewed the camp as relatively safe went into lockdown mode. They instituted new security protocols, and severely curtailed their activities. By the time the first bomb exploded that day in November, it was clear that Somalia's civil war had followed the refugees into exile.

Most of Asad's classmates ran to their homes. But curiosity pulled him in the opposite direction. He bounded through the heavy metal gate of the schoolyard and down a rutted sand track toward the site of the explosion. Soon he was gazing into a massive crater, six or eight feet in diameter. At its center was a blackened lump of metal, the largest remaining piece of what moments before had been a Toyota Land Cruiser. A crowd of onlookers formed around him, some of them shaken from the blast, others, he guessed, drawn as he had been by curiosity or the impulse to help. They shouted and jostled, their faces taut with emotion. Soon men in uniforms arrived. But they didn't rush to help the wounded, or to cordon off the scene. Instead they launched themselves at the bystanders, bludgeoning heads with wooden clubs and crunching ribs with heavy steel-toed boots. Terrified, Asad turned and headed for Room 101.

More bombs followed the first one in the coming weeks and

months, with each new episode triggering a round of indiscriminate reprisals from the police. Al-Shabab blew up several security convoys and assassinated two refugee leaders who had been elected to head up a community policing initiative in Dadaab. The police responded by raiding dozens of houses under the pretense of searching for weapons. They assaulted residents, stole and destroyed property. Some of the detainees were held for days, until family members could cobble together bribes of 10,000 shillings or more.

Having fled to Kenya for safety, the refugees suddenly found themselves caught between terrorists and a brutal, undisciplined police force. When one side lashed out at the other, Asad noticed that it was always ordinary refugees who paid the price. Making matters worse was the response of the aid agencies, which discontinued all but the most essential lifesaving services. Development and educational projects stalled. Food distribution was scaled back. In the schools there had always been a shortage of qualified teachers, but as fear descended on the camp, nearly all of the credentialed Kenyan teachers picked up and left. Those who remained were mainly so-called "incentive workers," perpetual interns drawn from the refugee population and paid only a nominal stipend because of Kenya's restrictive employment laws. "Classes became optional," Asad remembered. "You would go to school and no one would even be there."

Asad and his friends did their best to keep studying, retreating to Room 101 and trying to shut everything else out. But their parents fretted when they moved around the camp, and it was hard to focus when everyone around them was scared. Rumor had it that the exams would be cancelled anyway, because of the security threat. What if they had worked this hard for nothing? The question became difficult to ignore. By late 2011, when the group of friends had been teaching themselves for almost a year, it was clear that something would have to give.

IV

TAHRIB

Dadaab Refugee Camp, December 2011

The sand burned hot on Bekar's feet as he lingered in the backfield. Dusk had fallen over the barren soccer pitch, but the heat was still oppressive. It radiated up from the grass-less earth and hung thick in the air so that even shallow breaths threatened to overwhelm his lungs. From his position at center back, he kept the entire game in view, jogging forward when his teammates possessed the ball and falling back when they turned it over. Up two goals over rival club Al-Ahly, which drew its members from Block D1 of Ifo, Bekar should have felt enthused. Instead, he was sick with worry.

While he and his friends had been in Room 101 dreaming about the WUSC, two of his half-brothers, Abdirashid and Abdifata, had been plotting another way out of Dadaab. Nearly a decade older than him, both had wives and children back in Somalia. They didn't have the option of returning to school, and their prospects for employment in the camp were slim. Debt and anxiety mounting, they had begun to whisper about *tahrib*.

It was a word Bekar had heard often growing up, one that carried both the promise of fortune and the fear of death. An Arabic word traditionally used to describe the smuggling of illegal goods, *tahrib* in the Somali context had come to mean migration in search of work, usually without papers and usually to Europe or to the oil-rich monarchies of the Gulf. Young men were said to "go on *tahrib*," and as everyone in Dadaab knew, they went in large numbers. The more desperate you were, the more likely you were to try your luck abroad, knowing full well you might never come home.

In Dadaab, there were thousands of desperate people, and a thriving network of smugglers who could navigate the treacherous journey from Kenya, through South Sudan, Sudan, and Libya, across the Mediterranean to Italy. On the day Abdirashid and Abdifata had said their goodbyes, Bekar's third half-brother Zakariya also disappeared. He hadn't come home at sundown, and he hadn't turned up the next day. Unlike his two older brothers, he hadn't breathed a word about *tahrib*. But after a week had passed, no one doubted where he had gone.

His departure had come as a shock to Bekar, who had been closest with Zakariya. The two had seen each other practically every day since they arrived in Dadaab nearly five years ago. *He's my brother. How could he keep this one from me?* Bekar thought. Unlike Abdirashid and Abdifata, Zakariya wasn't married. Perhaps he thought his mother would forbid him from going with his brothers, since he didn't have a family to support. The unanswered questions gnawed at Bekar. He wondered if he should have said something, raised the subject directly with Zakariya during the period his other half-brothers had been discussing it. Now Zakariya was probably hundreds of miles away, packed in a crowded lorry or stuck in a migrant ghetto.

Bekar had tried his best to keep his mind on other things. In the last week alone, he had done hours of algebraic equations, working his way through a thick red textbook he shared with Asad and Abdi. During earlier periods of instability, he had found that the concentration required for mathematics had a steadying effect. Soccer offered another diversion. The match against Al-Ahly, he had hoped, would put his mind at ease at least for a few hours. But out on the pitch in the waning daylight hours, he felt himself transported across the desert to Sudan and Libya. The place he imagined was hot and harsh, even more desolate than Dadaab. It was teeming with the kinds of hazards he had heard awaited those who went on *tahrib*—wild animals, corrupt border agents, ruthless traffickers. He wondered whether Zakariya and the others could survive such a place.

...

Bekar was no stranger to uncertainty. Born in 1991, the year Siad Barre's dictatorship collapsed and Asad's family fled to Kenya, he was less than a week old when his father died of a mysterious fever. War and famine wracked the country that year and the next, while he lived with his mother, his father's other widow, and his seventeen siblings, in a squat four-bedroom house in Mogadishu. Dueling warlords carved up the capital around them, laying much of it to waste and killing thousands of people. Fighters wheeled through the streets in pickup trucks outfitted with heavy machine guns, looting stores and homes and clashing among themselves. Food stocks dwindled and prices soared. Soon thousands of people were starving across the country, their shrunken, skeletal bodies hauled away in "death trucks" that came for the deceased.

Aid workers tried to provide emergency relief to the sick and the hungry, but militants shook them down for cash and stole their supplies. UN peacekeepers eventually arrived, including thousands of American troops deployed as part of "Operation Restore Hope." But the foreign troops only accelerated Somalia's slide into chaos. When Bekar was two years old, U.S. forces attempted to capture warlord Mohammed Farah Aidid, triggering a two-day battle that ended with two Black Hawk helicopters downed and hundreds of Somalis and eighteen Americans dead. At the time, Bekar's family lived just a few blocks from Bakaara Market in Mogadishu's Black Sea district, where one of the U.S. choppers had crashed and where his mother ran a small shop selling cement and other construction wares. The market was the site of frequent skirmishes when he was growing up in the late 1990s and early 2000s, as warlords fought each other and against militias allied to a new movement of Islamic courts—groups of Muslim legal scholars that had the backing of the business community—that was gradually gaining sway.

Bekar managed to avoid most of the violence. But one day in early 2006, when he was thirteen years old, he was at school when the teachers abruptly dismissed the class. Rumors had circulated that fighting was about to break out between militiamen of the Islamic courts and one of the last remaining warlords. He thought about looking for his half-sister Sadia, who was studying at the same school, but as his classmates rushed past him for the door he decided there wasn't time. Bekar darted out into the street, zigzagging through the maze of narrow alleyways that led toward Bakaara Market. But everywhere he turned, roadblocks had suddenly appeared, manned by clan militias that he knew better than to cross. Heart racing, he backtracked and tried several alternate routes, crisscrossing the city in search of a safe path home. Eventually, he succeeded in making a wide berth around the fighting and circling back from the rear. When he burst through the door into the cool of the sitting room, his mother, Khadija, and his late father's second wife, Raaliyo, were both frantic.

"Where is your sister?" they wanted to know. "Why isn't she with you?"

Raaliyo's face was stricken with worry, and her dark eyes

searched his for answers. Bekar stood there speechless. There was nothing he could say to assuage her fear, no way to explain why he had reacted as he did. Before he could open his mouth, the door burst open a second time and in tumbled Sadia with one of her school friends. Raaliyo's face melted as she swept Sadia up in her arms.

. . .

Not long after that, a federation of Islamic courts finally imposed order on the wrecked capital city. They were backed by powerful clan militias and ruled by a harsh version of Islamic law. They banned pornography and music and even declared it a crime to watch the World Cup, forcing Bekar and his friends to listen to the 2006 World Cup matches on the BBC's Somali radio service. Thieves started having their hands amputated and women began to veil themselves in the style of more conservative Muslim societies. But the killing and the looting stopped, and for that most people were grateful. For the first time in more than a decade, the roads were clear of checkpoints. Commerce gradually resumed. It was among the only periods of sustained normalcy Bekar can remember, a time when he and his sisters walked to and from school without worry and the shop in Bakaara Market did well enough to put plenty of food on the table.

But the Islamic Courts Union had powerful enemies. Neighboring Ethiopia viewed it as a threat, as did the United States, which in the wake of the 9/11 attacks was eager to prevent Somalia from becoming a terrorist haven. In December 2006, the George W. Bush administration supported an Ethiopian invasion aimed at toppling the courts and installing a more pliant, internationally backed government. Thousands of Ethiopian troops marched on Mogadishu, backed by Russian-made tanks and fighter jets. They made quick work of the Islamic Courts militiamen, and within a few weeks they had taken control of the capital. Thousands of refugees streamed out of the city, headed for Ethiopia and Kenya.

Bekar's family had anticipated the devastation of the Ethiopian blitzkrieg and fled in an earlier wave, escaping the city before it became an inferno. They arrived in Dadaab around the time that Bekar should have been graduating from primary school, settling at first in Ifo, not far from the compound where Asad and his family lived. The two met in the sixth grade, after Bekar was sent back three grades on account of his poor English and Swahili. The two didn't become friends immediately, perhaps because Bekar was several years older than Asad. As he adjusted to life in the camp, Bekar mostly stuck together with his siblings. He was closest with Zakariya, who was two years his senior. They were practically inseparable, joining soccer matches whenever they could and playing cards together late into the evenings. But as the months passed and Bekar began to internalize the strange rhythms of Dadaab, he found himself drawn to the quiet, stammering boy who everyone in his class called The Professor.

He could sense in Asad the same drive to escape his circumstances that was beginning to develop in him. Life had never been easy in Mogadishu, but here it was hard in ways he hadn't previously imagined: the total dependence on others, the interminable waiting for everything. People lived as if they were saving a part of themselves for their real lives, which would presumably begin as soon as the war ended in Somalia or they were granted asylum in the United States. There were still weddings and births and funerals. People still laughed and loved and bickered. But to him, everything seemed half-hearted, diminished out of some shared subconscious need for self-preservation.

Asad didn't appear to live that way. He had thrown himself into his studies, grabbing tight to the one possibility without clear limits and using it to launch himself toward a future that, while still uncertain, had to be better than this. Bekar was determined to do the same, and their budding friendship revolved almost entirely around that shared goal. "In fact, we had one ambition. Our target was just to finish primary school and get good marks and then go to secondary school," Bekar recalled. "And once we got to secondary school, we had one target again: WUSC."

Bekar knew that wasn't all that animated his friend. Asad spent far too much time with his head in books that weren't assigned for class, books that would never help him pass his exams. Bekar tried reading some of them, but he never got past the opening pages. For him education had to serve a clear purpose—a scholarship, a degree, and someday, he hoped, a vocation. But if the two friends differed in their motivations, their objective was the same: getting out of Dadaab. "Because when people stay here in Dadaab, when they finish school, we could see they had nothing to do," Bekar said. "We decided, let us do something different from these other people."

. . .

Bekar's older siblings had taken the flight to Dadaab even harder than he had. There were odd jobs to be done in the camp—running deliveries, cleaning shops, digging pit latrines. But even the worst of these jobs were hard to get without clan or familial connections, and the line to fill them was long. Even harder to get were the "incentive worker" jobs at the international aid agencies and the UN. Those were virtually monopolized by the powerful clans.

Time and again Abdirashid and Abdifata failed in their efforts to find work. In the meantime, the calls from family back home grew more and more urgent. The Ethiopian invasion had shattered the fragile peace that took hold under the Islamic Courts Union and ignited a new insurgency—this one led by a militant wing of the ICU calling itself al-Shabab, or "the Youth." Al-Shabab targeted Ethiopian troops with suicide bombers and assassinations, turning Mogadishu into a war zone once again. They also press-ganged young men into service as fighters and religious police, enforcing an even stricter religious code than the ICU. Soon the group controlled the bulk of southern Somalia and all but a few square blocks of the capital city, where the embattled transitional government was hunkered down. Al-Shabab's fighters were ruthless, and their tactics—including blocking foreign shipments of emergency aid—helped fuel the famine that by 2011 was forcing thousands of new refugees to flee to Dadaab.

Abdirashid and Abdifata were running out of options. And with al-Shabab beginning to terrorize Dadaab, forcing many of the big aid agencies to scale back or pull out, the chances of finding work were growing slimmer by the day. And so Abdirashid and Abdifata talked their plan over with the family. "They said, 'Instead of staying here not doing anything, let us go on *tahrib*. We either die or we get something,'" Bekar remembered. Khadija and Raaliyo—"the two moms," as Bekar called them—listened quietly as his half-brothers made their case. Neither woman tried to dissuade them. With no good options, there was hardly a counterargument to be made. But he could tell they were worried, that they were holding something back when at last they nodded and said, "All the best."

Bekar had resigned himself to the loss of two of his half-brothers. He understood why they were willing to risk everything to provide for their families. But why Zakariya had gone with them—that he couldn't fathom. Just the other week, the two of them had watched Manchester United play at the cinema in Bosnia, an improvised establishment that consisted of a projector and an old sheet housed under a rusty tin roof. Afterward, they had hoofed it back home in the dark, half giddy, half scared, when a hyena emerged from the shadows, its eyes glowing green in the night.

Now instead of laughing, Bekar imagined Zakariya weak with exhaustion in the desert. Bekar's anxiety mounted with each passing day, pooling in the space between his ribs where his appetite had once been. He could see that the two moms were also worried. They whispered to each other more than usual, and they said little to anyone else. Every once in a while, Raaliyo would check her mobile phone, thumbing the translucent rubber keys to light up the small yellow screen. He recognized the look on her face each time she did it. He had seen it before, on the day Mogadishu had erupted with violence and he had run home without his half-sister Sadia.

Six weeks after Zakariya disappeared, Raaliyo's phone finally rang. All three brothers had made it safely to Europe, three of roughly 62,000 migrants whose arrival in Italy by sea that year would coincide with the first wave of refugees fleeing the civil war in Syria. It was an early harbinger of the coming crisis in the Mediterranean, unleashed by the collapse of strongman regimes across the Middle East and made more dangerous by the fortress mentality of many European countries. As record numbers claimed asylum on the continent, the European Union scrambled to secure its borders, shoring up remaining dictatorships like Sudan and Ethiopia with aid in exchange for promises to crack down on human smugglers, and earmarking billions for development under the theory that it would deter migration. Little distinction was made between economic migrants and refugees. The goal was to stanch the flow.

In Dadaab, people measured the crisis not by numbers of refugees, or even deaths at sea, but by the silent disappearance of loved ones. Friends would simply stop showing up for school. Neighbors would vanish without a trace. But as the years wore on and more and more of their journeys were documented on social media, it became clear just how lucky Zakariya and his brothers had been. Everyone had seen the videos, posted to Facebook and shared on WhatsApp, of shackled migrants, often bruised and bleeding, pleading for relatives to send money to their torturers. Evidence of extortion and even slavery was everywhere, but still more people decided to go. *Either we die, or we get something*, they must have thought. Bekar never considered going on *tahrib*, but he didn't disagree with the logic.

V

STRIKING OUT

Dadaab Refugee Camp–Nairobi, Kenya, December 2011

The pronouncement from Sharif came without warning. One day toward the end of 2011, the old man announced that it was time for Asad to get married. He believed that the institution of marriage helped settle young men. And once he had reached a decision about something—anything—the family knew better than to try to talk him out of it. Now, more than a decade after his sister had run away to Nairobi to avoid an arranged marriage, sixteen-year-old Asad faced the same impossible choice. With another two years of high school ahead of him and the promise of Canada beckoning after that, he wasn't ready to get married and start a family of his own. But defying Sharif didn't feel like an option either. He knew he wouldn't be able to look his father in the eye after that.

The only thing to do was leave for a time as Maryan had

done. But go where? Nairobi was risky without papers and in any case it was too expensive. His little excursion to Eastleigh had made that clear. Maryan had taken his side in the marriage dispute and offered to pay his tuition at a school outside the camp. But he knew she was struggling financially and having problems with her husband. It wouldn't be fair to ask her for more than he believed she could afford. Several older refugees he was friendly with had received scholarships to attend a boarding school in Garissa, but when he reached out to people he knew with connections there, he kept hitting dead ends. He didn't have any other close family members living outside of Dadaab, but there was one cousin, the daughter of one of Kaltuma's brothers, who had managed to buy a *kitambulisho* from a corrupt civil servant. Her name was Idil and she had moved her family nearly 500 miles away, to Kisii, a town in southwest Kenya not far from Lake Victoria. Her husband worked as an M-Pesa agent there, helping people send and receive mobile money. They had a baby daughter and a small two-room house.

When Asad told Bekar and Abdi that he planned to go to Kisii they were shocked. For nearly two years, the three of them had been focused on preparing for the WUSC. They had made a pact to help each other, to be the educational support system that was missing in Dadaab. The surge in al-Shabab attacks had certainly made things more difficult, but none of them were ready to give up. What was more, moving across the country without first securing admission to a new school struck his friends as a big risk, especially since he would have to dodge the police on the way.

But Bekar and Abdi had spent enough time around Sharif to know that he wasn't likely to back down on something as important as marriage. When Asad told them that things had reached a breaking point, they seemed to understand. The three friends agreed to keep in touch on a mobile group chat, and to continue tutoring one another as best they could. From now on, though, Asad would go it alone.

. . .

Kisii was green and hilly, a highland sanctuary of tall trees and modest tin-roofed homes that thundered loudly in the rain. Idil and her husband moved with the baby into one room and invited Asad to take the other. He did odd jobs around the house to pitch in, cooking meals and fetching water from the tap as he had done back in Ifo. But with no income besides what Maryan was able to send from time to time, he fretted about being a burden on his hosts.

School was another problem. The only place he could afford was Daraja Mbili, a bare-bones establishment originally set up to educate orphans, many of whom had lost parents to the HIV epidemic that ravaged the region around Lake Victoria in the 1980s and early 1990s. The sturdy cement classrooms and heavy wooden desks were better than Towfiq's, but there was still no library and no laboratory equipment. None of his new classmates had all of the required textbooks. They also viewed him with suspicion.

Kisii was interior Kenya, and he could immediately sense that he was an outsider. The terrorist attacks in and around Dadaab might have been hundreds of miles away, but they had stoked fear across the entire country. Asad was the only Somali student in the school, and quite possibly the only Somali in the town aside from Idil and her husband. He told no one that he was a refugee, not even his teachers or the headmaster. Doing so could have jeopardized his freedom. But he couldn't hide his Somali features, and from his first day at Daraja Mbili the other kids were taunting him and calling him al-Shabab.

He sought refuge where he had so often in the past—in the stories he read and, increasingly, those that he wrote. Even before the falling out with Sharif had forced him to leave home, he had been writing short stories and book reviews. He modeled them after what he read in the newspapers that he found at the butcher shop in Bosnia. There was a pullout in the *Daily Nation* dedicated to African literature that appeared once a week. He loved finding that section, and after reading it he was often inspired to write his own reviews of books in the library at Ifo Secondary. One day, he noticed a call for submissions that listed a generic email address. He began sending in his articles, hoping he might find them printed in the next literary supplement to arrive with a shipment of meat.

None of his articles ever made it back to Ifo, but in Kisii the newspapers were delivered every day. One day in May 2013, after he had been at Daraja Mbili for a little more than four months, he submitted a different kind of article to the *Daily Nation*. For months, a national debate had been playing out in the newspapers about the reading culture in Kenya and whether it was in decline. Students, more than one writer lamented, no longer seemed to appreciate the literary arts. "[I]f you want to hide anything from a Kenyan, put it in a book," one columnist opined. As a high school student whose intensifying workload was cutting into his other intellectual pursuits, Asad had something to say on the subject. "I write on behalf of the high school students who have been an object of ridicule in the newspapers of late. We have been blamed for the waning reading culture," he wrote in a terse letter to the editor. "Dear professors, teachers, writers, and journalists, did you stop to think what has forced us to abandon books? . . . Fear of exams is gnawing away at our souls."

To his surprise, the letter appeared in the *Daily Nation*'s May 11 edition, under the headline "Blame the Curriculum for Poor Book Habits." And to his even greater surprise, the Ministry of Education issued an official rebuttal on its website, blaming students and teachers—anyone but its own bureaucrats who had designed the Kenyan course of study. It was surreal. Here he was living in hiding, unworthy of even an ID card. Yet somehow he merited an individual response from the highest level of government? But the real shock came days later, when a school administrator handed him a scrap of paper with an email address and the name David Ongwae scribbled on it.

Ongwae had grown up in Kisii County. By the time he read Asad's letter to the editor, he was a successful lawyer living in South Africa. Moved to do something for the students of Daraja Mbili, he promised to donate 1,000 books, as well as a computer, a printer, and other electronics for a new library. Asad was flabbergasted. One thousand books was more than the whole library at Ifo Secondary. Ever since he began sneaking in at night to read, he had entertained the fantasy of someday finishing every book in the world. He had lately begun to doubt that this was possible, but a gift of this size would surely bring him close. It would also show his new classmates that Somalis were capable of more than violence and hatred. After all, the new library would be named after him. On the day it finally opened, in August 2013, he wrote a Facebook post tagging Bekar and ten other friends: "Being the only Somali student in the school, I think I am leaving behind a legacy. In the future, when another Somali student joins the school, he will not be called a terrorist, but instead respected."

He and Ongwae kept in regular contact, striking up a correspondence that would last for nearly two years. The older man proffered advice and often shared his views on politics—some of which struck Asad as wise and some of which he thought were narrow-minded. He kept his opinions to himself, though, and only divulged bits and pieces of his backstory. Ongwae seemed to think he had been born in Kisii, and Asad didn't correct him or share anything about his childhood in Dadaab. "I told him parts of my story, but I didn't tell him everything," he said. "I didn't want to make an enemy."

Ongwae also sent money: 10,000 shillings, or $100, a month to help with expenses and school fees. It was a godsend for Asad, who was dead broke by then and unable to ask his sister for any more than she was already sending. Now at least he could take care of himself. But even as he began to feel more at ease in Kisii, Dadaab kept reeling him back in.

• • •

Although there had been no real movement on their resettlement case for almost a decade, the family's case number still appeared from time to time on the bulletin board outside the UNHCR field office in Ifo. No one ever called or came to say you were scheduled for an interview or a medical exam, so you had to check the board week after week, month after month—and in this case, year after year. Whenever No. 525765 appeared, one of Asad's younger siblings would call or text, and he would make the long and risky trek back to the camp. Missing an appointment could set the whole family's prospects of resettlement back, even if those prospects looked increasingly grim. Every once in a while, he would email Church World Services, the U.S. State Department contractor in charge of vetting candidates for resettlement, to inquire about the status of their case. Most of the time no one replied, but whenever someone did, the response was always the same: "Your case is pending for medical examinations."

The trips back to Dadaab were never efficient. It took two or three days to get back and forth from Kisii, and the appointments rarely happened on time, the result of an overburdened bureaucracy riddled with corruption. Often Asad had to wait around for days or even weeks, missing classes and exams back at school. Since he couldn't tell his teachers about his refugee status, there was no way to explain away his frequent absences. As far as he could tell, they only tolerated his poor attendance record because his letter to the editor had brought the school a new library. Still, Dadaab gave him something Daraja Mbili could not: material for his budding journalistic and literary ambitions.

His earliest writings had closely mirrored what he read in the literary supplement: book reviews, meditations on language and literature. But as the political atmosphere became more intensely polarized, and as refugees and Somalis came increasingly under attack, he felt compelled to write about the world into which he had been born. Often, his subjects were women, and their stories tended to highlight the severe social and cultural constraints they faced. Looking back on it, Maryan's example certainly informed these choices, as did the experience of being surrounded by women as a child. As the only boy fetching water and wood in Ifo, he had seen what women daily endured in a society that expected them to serve and obey. "That gives you a different perspective on life," he recalled. "You say, 'What are we doing to our women?'"

By then he was writing for multiple outlets. One was a magazine run entirely by refugees and funded by the humanitarian nonprofit FilmAid. Another was an online journal called *Sahan* that was started by an informal group of Somali intellectuals, some of them in Kenya and some in Canada and the United States. He had connected with the editors online, exchanging emails and Facebook messages and eventually traveling to Nairobi to meet a few of them in person. In one article that appeared in both publications, he profiled a young woman named Halima who sold tea by the cup. She had been forced into an arranged marriage and then abandoned after four months, "left penniless and pregnant" as she tried to support eleven siblings. She reminded Asad of Maryan, who had faced similar obstacles and also chose to sacrifice her own happiness for her brothers and sisters. "Dadaab was not a nurturing home for girls," he wrote, observing that "early marriages and house chores snuffed out their talents."

He also wrote about women who overcame such obstacles. After the *Daily Nation* published his letter to the editor, the newspaper began accepting more of his story ideas. For one he interviewed Fatuma Omar Ismail, a twenty-year-old engineering student who had scored an A− on her national exam and won the coveted WUSC. Born in Somalia before the civil war "gobbled up" all that her family had, she had fled to Dadaab as a young child. "All around her she could see people barely surviving, young and old beaten by the vagaries of a refugee camp," Asad wrote. But Fatuma's father believed in the power of education and had encouraged her to study hard in school. "He told her that everything was possible, that she could break away from the yoke of refugee life if she wanted, and that books were her only hope out of the squalor she had known all her life."

Asad could have been writing about himself—or about any of his friends back in Room 101. A few weeks after he interviewed Fatuma, in October 2014, they all took the exam they had been preparing for diligently for the last four years. A high score would be their ticket out of Dadaab; a low one could be a life sentence to its confines—or at least to a lifetime of running from the authorities. Asad knew that all the missed classes had left him at a disadvantage, but he had read the study guides from cover to cover and taken dozens of practice tests using past exam questions dating back to 1990. He knew the material inside out. The exams were administered by subject, and staggered over the course of more than a week. An overall grade of B+ was all he needed to qualify for the WUSC. And when he walked out of his last exam he felt confident, like that was a foregone conclusion.

There had been other triumphs during his Daraja Mbili

years that seemed like good omens. He had won a national essay writing competition put on by Riara University in Nairobi, collecting a 50,000-shilling first-prize check that he was unable to cash for lack of a bank account. The editors of the *Daily Nation* had invited him to the newsroom for a three-week internship, during which he worked on his beloved literary supplement. At the end of the internship, a bald and bespectacled editor named Eric Obino had offered to hire him full-time when he finished high school, provided he could secure a *kitambulisho*. It felt like he was finally on a roll. "I was assured almost that I would get the WUSC," he remembered. "It was like I knew already, like it was my destiny."

The exam results were transmitted by text message, lighting up his black Nokia smartphone one day in March 2015. But they were not what he had expected. His overall grade, a C+, registered like a blow to the abdomen. He was alone in Room 101 as he processed the news, having returned from Kisii a few months earlier and moved into Bekar's family compound. All around him on the dirt floor lay evidence of mental exertion: binders, notebooks, worn paperbacks he had amassed over the years. Scrawled on the metal door was the poem by William Ernest Henley, lines that seemed like they were taunting him now.

I am the master of my fate,
I am the captain of my soul.

He thought about Bekar and Abdi, both of whom must be reading their exam results now too. He thought also about David Ongwae, who had asked for the results as soon as they had been published. Ongwae had believed in him and invested in his future. Now there would be no WUSC, no Canada, no life outside the prisonlike camp where he had been born. Here in Dadaab, it turned out you couldn't outrun your past. The same misfortune that brought you here would also seal your fate. He switched off his phone and retreated into the darkness.

...

Just before dawn a few weeks later, on April 2, 2015, al-Shabab militants carried out the deadliest terrorist attack on Kenyan soil since the 1998 U.S. Embassy bombing. Masked gunmen stormed the campus of Garissa University College, about sixty miles from Dadaab, just as students were waking up for class. Armed with AK-47s and wearing suicide vests, they shot their way through the dormitories, leaving a bloody trail of corpses in their wake. Fifteen hours later, when the standoff with the police and military finally ended, 152 people were dead, including four of the assailants.

The attack unleashed a new wave of anti-Somali vitriol in the press. It also sparked an exchange with Ongwae, who often shared his thoughts on the news in their emailed correspondence. He seemed to like that Asad was writing regularly for various newspapers, and sometimes offered suggestions for what to write about—suggestions that Asad always politely ignored. On this occasion, Ongwae thought he should write an apology on behalf of all Somalis for the brutal massacre. Asad was taken aback, angry and hurt that his mentor saw him as in any way responsible. Did he really think every Somali secretly sympathized with al-Shabab? Did he think it was Asad's responsibility to denounce what was plainly the work of bloodthirsty extremists? "I'm not a terrorist. I'm not going to apologize for terrorists attacking Kenya," he remembered telling Ongwae.

Things deteriorated from there. Tensions had already been mounting over little requests that Asad had left unanswered. Ongwae had asked to see his progress reports even before the national exam, but Asad had missed so many classes traveling back to Dadaab that he didn't have any. He had also failed to follow up with some of Ongwae's business associates, after the older man had gone out of his way to introduce them. The last straw had been the C+ on the national exam. Ongwae clearly viewed that as not just a personal failure but as a rebuke of his own generosity. Harsh words were exchanged. And then an email with the subject line "Private and Confidential" landed in Asad's inbox. In it, Ongwae lambasted Asad's "strange normative values" and "selfish self-centered characteristics," making clear that their relationship had run its course. "You listen but you do not hear. . . . You are not half as clever or as wise as you think," the email read in part.

The letter would have a lasting impact, setting in motion a

series of events that Ongwae couldn't have foreseen and surely didn't intend. It reached a vulnerability Asad didn't know he had, cutting deeper into his self-confidence and leaving him more shaken than any previous stumble. His exam results had already left him feeling as if he had failed everyone he cared about—his sister, his parents, teachers, and friends. "I didn't become who they wanted me to be," he remembered. But seeing it spelled out in those terms caused him to fall apart. "That broke me. That literally changed me," he said. "That was the first time in my life where I was like, 'It's not worth it.'"

VI

HELP FROM AFAR

Dadaab Refugee Camp–Richland, Washington, April 2016

The sight of her father lying slumped on the ground was more than Maryan could stomach. Beads of sweat quivered on his tall, domed forehead, and his shrunken chest rattled noisily as it heaved slowly up and down. Above him, the twisted branches of a prickly acacia tree extended an uneven patchwork of shade. To ease the midsummer heat, Sharif, who was now in his late seventies and suffering from recurrent tuberculosis, had taken to dousing his pillow with water. But it kept drying out every hour or so and he would have to douse it again.

It had been five years since Maryan fled to Seattle, only to have her husband chase after her less than a month later. After that they had been on again, off again, moving frequently and bouncing from job to job. Maryan had had two more children, become a U.S. citizen, and finally divorced Yussuf in 2012—after filing a restraining order against him. Somewhere along the line, she had given up on her parents' resettlement case and decided to go back and see them as soon as she could save up the money.

Now in the spring of 2016, she was standing in a place that was at once unchanged and unrecognizable. Dadaab was as it had always been, full of trash and dust and shabby ersatz huts—a permanent temporary city. Yet whole new sections of the camp had been added in her absence, and parts of Block A4 where she had played as a child had since been parceled into compounds for more recent arrivals. When she had returned to their old compound with Asad, she felt disoriented, like the passage of time had rearranged things without moving them forward. Even her own family felt full of strangers: a sibling she had never met and others she couldn't recognize, parents who had never seen their grandchildren.

In the brief time she had been back, she had tried in vain to reestablish a connection. She and Asad had gone on long walks around the camp, snapping photos on her tablet and dredging up old memories. Things had not gone as planned for her brother, and she could tell he was struggling to cope with the disappointments of the last year. He had found work as a substitute teacher at Ifo Secondary, teaching English to students more hopeful about the future than he. But he seemed sullen and aimless, like he had lost that inquisitive spark that had always set him apart from the other kids. "He had all these dreams and hopes, and they all faded out," Maryan remembered. When she relayed her concerns to her mother, Kaltuma confided that she was afraid he might go on *tahrib*.

Maryan did her best to sound upbeat. She tried to get her brother to talk about his goals, and when that failed, she reminded him of the virtues of patience. But even as she tried to reassure him, Maryan felt overcome with despair. Being in the United States, it had been possible to believe that things had gotten better in Dadaab, that it wasn't just her own life that had improved. But seeing her family in the same wretched condition she had left them added a new layer of pain to their decade of separation. Not only were they trapped in a place so hopeless that hundreds were leaving it for war-torn Libya, there now seemed a real possibility that her father might die here after nearly a quarter century of waiting. There was no way for him to see a doctor, and Maryan worried about the quality of the medicines her siblings bought for him in Bosnia. It was impossible to tell if the drugs were authentic, or if their expired labels had rendered them useless.

What was clear to Maryan was that she couldn't allow her parents to remain here much longer. Two years prior, in April 2014, she had filed the initial paperwork to sponsor them for green cards—a long, complicated, and expensive process that would allow them to join her in the United States. She couldn't afford to sponsor her siblings, but she had hoped to at least bring Sharif and Kaltuma to a place where there was adequate medical care. Seeing her father suffering like this, though, she knew she was running out of time. "My dad isn't safe here," she remembered thinking. "Whatever it takes, I'm going to take him to America."

...

For the previous four years, Maryan and her kids had lived in Richland, a quiet town of single-story bungalows and white picket fences in southeastern Washington. Known as "Atomic Town, U.S.A.," Richland is home to the Manhattan Project complex that produced the plutonium for one of the bombs dropped on Nagasaki during World War II. It is now the most contaminated nuclear site in the United States, but its residents seemed to embrace their proximity to environmental disaster. Stores with names like Atomic City Thrift and Nuclear Care Partners line the streets, and restaurants serve specials like Fallout Fajitas and Reactor Core Pizza. The high school where Maryan planned to send her kids had as its official logo a billowing mushroom cloud.

The predominantly white town of 50,000 was an unlikely place for a family of Somali immigrants—but that was exactly why she chose it. In his bid to control Maryan, Yussuf had once again turned much of the Somali community against her during the short time they lived in Seattle, at one point ginning up a full-blown scandal over her decision to wear winter boots. (Somalis traditionally wear sandals, and her embrace of Western footwear had been taken as a sign of loose morals.) So in one of their periods of separation, she had moved the kids to a town where she knew she wouldn't feel trapped in an insular immigrant community. She wanted neighbors who wouldn't scrutinize her every move, and in the low-slung housing project on Pike Avenue she finally had them. When she decided to attempt an end-run around the broken UN resettlement process, however, it was to a relief agency that worked mainly with refugees that she turned for the name of an immigration attorney.

Wendy Hernandez's office was on a quiet tree-lined street in Walla Walla, about an hour west of Richland. She was blunt with Maryan when she discussed her parents' plight. A former nurse and mental health counselor who helped establish one of the only immigration law clinics in eastern Washington, she explained that abandoning the UN route would mean shouldering all of the burdens herself. Whereas refugees don't have to cover the administrative costs of resettlement and are eligible for government benefits when they arrive, green card recipients are the financial responsibility of their sponsors. What that meant in practice was that Maryan would have to pay out of pocket for every step of the application process, and also prove that she was capable of supporting her parents financially. Not only would she have to sign an affidavit promising to reimburse the government for any welfare benefits they might claim in the future, she would have to show that her annual income and assets exceeded 125 percent of the federal poverty level for a family of eight—or $50,112 in 2014.

If Maryan could find a cosponsor, she and that person could combine their incomes to meet the threshold together, Wendy explained. It was best if the cosponsor was a family member, but he or she didn't have to be. Anyone who was willing to sign the affidavit would do, provided they were a citizen or a permanent resident. Maryan left the office feeling demoralized. The previous year, she had earned a little more than $20,000. And now that she was a single mother, she wasn't sure she would be able to find anyone willing to make such a generous promise.

So Maryan did the only thing she could think of—she set about finding more work. She already had a full-time job at a state agency called Aging and Long Term Care, which provided in-home care for seniors. She worked forty hours a week there as a certified nursing assistant, bathing and feeding elderly patients, and taking their vital signs. When a company called Professional Case Management advertised for part-time CNAs in her area, she picked up three additional night shifts, each twelve hours long. PCM billed itself as "the nation's premier care provider for nuclear weapons and uranium workers." It was a quintessentially Richland job if there ever was one. She would come home just before dawn, sleep for maybe an hour, and then drag herself out of bed to make breakfast for the kids. She would try to ask them each at least one question in the brief moments she had with them every morning, before they went off to school and she reported for her day job at Aging and Long Term Care.

From his teachers, Maryan had heard that Mohamed was turning into a prankster—a "captivating comedian," as one of them memorably put it—while Ambia, two years younger, had grown into her mother's little helper, the one deputized to make household decisions while she was away at work. Ambia reminded Maryan of a younger version of herself, always mediating between her siblings (the household rules taped above the fridge named her as permanent holder of the remote) and picking up slack when her mother wasn't able. Maryan was grateful to have a daughter she could count on, but worried she was missing too much of all of her children's lives. Just keeping track of the day-to-day necessities was a struggle. If they ran out of milk or cereal or anything else, she would write a note on the back of her hand, so she wouldn't forget in her permanent state of exhaustion.

On the days when she didn't work the night shift, she would sometimes squeeze in an hour or two of translation work with a firm called Northwest Interpreters, Inc. "I lost almost sixty pounds because I wasn't sleeping," she remembered. "I was working, working, working."

But the more she worked, the more it felt like she was falling behind. At the beginning of 2014, she had received roughly $700 in food stamps every month through the federal government's

Supplemental Nutrition Assistance Program. But after she started working the second job, and her reported income increased, her benefits were slashed to roughly $400 per month. At the same time, the rent for their apartment more than doubled, the result of Section 8 housing assistance designed to keep recipients' rent steady at approximately 30 percent of their income. With a family of six to support in Dadaab and five kids of her own, though, it felt like the tide kept rising another inch every time she managed to get her head above water.

And that was before the fees associated with her parents' green card applications. To her surprise, Maryan was able to find a cosponsor. Muktar Abdulle was a friend of a friend, a naturalized citizen like her who lived in nearby Pasco, one of the Tri-Cities along with Richland and Kennewick. He had no family to support, and a job that paid $15.45 an hour at a company called Conagra Foods. When Maryan first approached him, he had shrugged her off. But she had worn him down over a period of months, telling him about her father's poor health and about the abysmal conditions in Dadaab. In April 2014, Wendy filed visa petitions for Sharif and Kaltuma with Maryan and Muktar listed as cosponsors. The cost was $840—plus $900 in legal fees.

In October, they got word that Sharif's petition had been approved. His application was advanced to the visa processing center, a step that involved more forms and associated costs: an immigrant visa fee of $325, an affidavit support fee of $120.

Meanwhile, U.S. Citizenship and Immigration Services sent a notice of "intent to deny" Kaltuma's petition. The agency needed more evidence that she was actually Maryan's mother. Wendy and Maryan spent the next year or so gathering more affidavits, by which point Sharif's application had timed out and Maryan had to pay the visa and affidavit support fees once again. By mid-2016, when her parents' cases were finally sent to the consular staff at the U.S. Embassy in Nairobi, where the final visa decisions are made, she had paid another $2,990, including legal fees.

...

Not long after Maryan returned home from Dadaab, and around the time Sharif's and Kaltuma's green card applications finally made it to the decision makers at the U.S. Embassy, the family faced yet another dilemma. In May 2016, the Kenyan government announced that it planned to close Dadaab, as well as another large refugee camp on its western border, because of security concerns. It had long claimed that the camp harbored terrorists, including those who had planned a bloody 2013 attack on a Nairobi shopping mall in which sixty-seven people were slaughtered. No evidence for this claim had ever been furnished, but it served as a handy pretext for the government's periodic threats to shutter the camp and expel its hundreds of thousands of residents.

Unlike with the previous threats to close Dadaab, the government followed this one up with action. It disbanded the

Department of Refugee Affairs, effectively barring new refugees from registering for assistance. Then it announced plans to move at least 150,000 people out of the camp by the end of the year, mainly by returning them to Somalia. No one would be forcibly uprooted, it claimed, but officials declined to say what would happen to refugees who wanted to stay. Ominously, the government appointed several army generals to the committee tasked with closing Dadaab. Stay after the November 30 deadline for closure, it seemed to be saying, and risk being caught up in a military operation to close the camp.

The uncertainty added to Maryan's long list of worries. She knew that Kenyan security forces had rounded up and deported hundreds of ethnic Somalis in recent years, dumping them back in Mogadishu even if they were registered refugees. From her brother, she heard the rumors that were spreading in the camp: The army was about to begin bulldozing people's homes. Anyone who remained risked being loaded into trucks and driven across the border. Since 2014, the UN had been running a voluntary repatriation program. It offered free transportation and a small resettlement package—usually a blanket, a mat to sleep on, and roughly $200—to anyone willing to return to Somalia. Initially, it had few takers. But as the terrifying rumors coursed through Dadaab, more people began to raise their hands. Soon, the UN was repatriating as many as 1,000 people a day.

The UN claimed that Somalia was safe for return, but much of the country remained a war zone. African Union forces, fighting a bloody, block-by-block counterinsurgency campaign, had recaptured most of Mogadishu and other major urban areas from al-Shabab. But the al Qaeda–linked militants still controlled most of rural southern and central Somalia. And they continued to strike at will virtually anywhere in the country, assassinating journalists, politicians, and ordinary civilians who dared to defy their strict religious codes. The militants had attacked a famous hotel less than a block from the presidential palace three times in the last two years, most recently killing twenty-two people with a truck bomb. Nowhere in Somalia was beyond al-Shabab's reach, the militants had made clear. No one who opposed them could ever be truly safe.

For months, the family debated what to do. Like many refugees, they were afraid that by declining the UN's offer they risked being left with nothing. But they also knew that returning to Somalia would mean giving up any chance of ever being reunited as a family. They would lose their refugee status, and with it any hope of resettlement.

Then one day in late November Maryan got word that her parents had finally been scheduled for an appointment at the U.S. Embassy on December 6. It was the last phase of the visa application process, and it meant that they would need to report to the embassy in Nairobi in person, as well as for one last medical check. The decision had been made for them, it seemed. Asad would move Sharif and Kaltuma to Eastleigh until their travel documents were ready. Once they were safely on their way to Washington, they would decide where Asad and his two younger siblings would go.

For $500, which Maryan sent, Asad managed to secure a temporary travel authorization for his parents, allowing them to pass through the police checkpoint where he had been detained years ago. For another $50 a week, he rented them a room with two twin beds at the Makka Al-Mukarramah, a hostel in Eastleigh that catered to Somali travelers. Neither of their parents spoke English or even Swahili, so he had to chaperone them everywhere, doing all of their shopping and guiding them to and from the nearby Jamia mosque every day. Even with their travel papers, moving around Eastleigh was risky. Maryan knew they were likely to be singled out for bribes, and she worried that the frantic pace of life in Nairobi would overwhelm her father. She checked in with Asad as often as she could, but she could sense there were things he wasn't telling her. With so many other parts of his life in disarray, he had thrown himself into the task of caring for their parents, and she could tell that he was doing as much as he could on his own so as to lessen the load on her shoulders.

More setbacks were on the horizon, however. Their parents completed their final medical checks, but for some reason Kaltuma's results weren't sent to the embassy in time for her interview, delaying her case once again while Sharif's proceeded to the next stage. Then Maryan got word that the U.S.

government was still questioning whether Kaltuma was really her mother. Both of them would have to undergo DNA testing to prove that they were in fact related. Maryan would have to pay for her own test in Richland, and then for her mother's test in Nairobi—$400 each plus a specimen collection fee of $45. When the results were ready, she would have to pay another $200 to transmit them to the U.S. Embassy.

By now Maryan was deep in debt. Unable to keep up with the endless stream of expenses, she had borrowed money from friends and racked up thousands of dollars in credit card debt. As the interest payments mounted, they had started to feel theoretical—so large they couldn't be real. She had no idea how she would ever pay it all back. All she knew was she had to keep going. By January 2017, though, it seemed as if the waiting period was finally drawing to an end. The DNA test kits had yet to be sent to Kenya, but Wendy was confident that they would eventually put the government's doubts to rest. Sharif, meanwhile, had sailed through his medical check, having completed a course of antibiotics for his tuberculosis, and was expecting to be called for his final visa interview any day now. Then on January 27, President Donald Trump's eighth day in office, he signed an executive order that changed everything.

. . .

Prior to Executive Order 13769, which temporarily suspended all refugee admissions to the United States and barred entry to travelers from seven Muslim-majority countries, including Somalia, Maryan hadn't paid much attention to Donald Trump. She had caught glimpses of his orange face on television and on the cover of magazines, but she had been too busy trying to stay afloat to worry much about the candidate who called for a "total and complete shutdown of Muslims entering the United States." But as news of the travel ban spread like wildfire that afternoon, Maryan suddenly realized that she was a target of his administration. She called Asad in Eastleigh and sobbed into the receiver: "Why now? Why me? What did we ever do wrong to deserve this?"

In the days and weeks that followed, she stayed glued to the television. She watched as analysts debated the legality of the ban, and as news anchors reported various challenges in the courts. She cheered when a federal judge in Seattle temporarily blocked the executive order, and cried when Trump signed a second one a month later, limiting the scope of the ban but still targeting Somalis. The legal landscape seemed to shift daily, and as closely as she followed the news, Maryan could never answer the most important question: What does this mean for us?

It was agony, the waiting without answers. When she wasn't watching CNN, Maryan texted with other refugees or combed through social media for information about people in similar situations. No one could say for sure whether oversees embassies were still processing visa applications, or if the entire immigration apparatus had ground to a halt. She was so consumed by the news cycle that Ambia had to eventually stage an intervention. She said, "You got to stop watching this, Mom. It's making you crazy."

The travel ban was having other ripple effects as well. In the twelve years she had been in America, Maryan could recall only a single overt experience with racism. At St. Joseph's Hospital in Tucson, a manager had sent her home for wearing a hijab; apparently the dress code forbade headwear. But when she had reported the incident to a superior, he had been apologetic and ordered special hijab covers made for her out of the same synthetic fabric as hospital scrubs. What a wonderful country, Maryan had thought at the time. Something like that would never have happened in Kenya. But as the national debate around the travel ban grew more intense, and as Trump's followers grew more emboldened, she began to sense a change come over the community. It wasn't that her white neighbors looked at her differently, although one woman at the playground did ask if she was "sad that she was alone," being one of the only people in town who was "different." But as hate crimes against Muslims began to appear regularly in the news, the few other Somali families she had met in Richland started to whisper about moving to Seattle. It's no longer safe here, they said. Best to move to a big city full of immigrants where there would be strength in numbers. Within a few months, most of them had picked up and left.

Maryan decided to stay. She had had enough of tight-knit

Somali communities, and she had never felt unwelcome in Richland. On the contrary, she had been stunned by the generosity of some of the people she had met there. Her son's music teacher, a sweet middle-aged woman named Pam Wheatley, must have sensed that Maryan was barely keeping it together during the period she was working double shifts. She had a way of showing up to lend a hand when things were at their worst—whether it was a sick child or a missed appointment or an overdue rent payment. Pam never forgot a birthday, and every year on the first day of school, she would appear with bundles of school supplies. When Wendy had first explained that Maryan would need a cosponsor for her parents' green card applications, Pam had been the first person who came to mind. But it turned out that she was already cosponsoring her daughter's husband, who was a Norwegian citizen. "I would do it for you," she had told Maryan at the time, "but I'm doing it for my daughter."

By early March, a window of opportunity had opened up in which it seemed possible that her father's visa might come through. An appeals court had upheld the Seattle judge's order blocking key parts of the first travel ban, and Trump's second travel ban, signed on March 6, wasn't due to come into effect until 12:01 a.m. on March 16. Wendy had been corresponding directly with the embassy on Maryan's behalf, trying to expedite both Sharif's and Kaltuma's cases so that they could get out before the deadline. Sometime before March 9, Wendy received word that Sharif's visa would be ready for collection the following day. But when he and Asad went to pick it up, he was informed that it was still being processed. Then on March 14, Wendy received an email from Customer Service Representative 7 of the Embassy's Immigrant Visa Unit, saying that unfortunately Sharif's visa had been "recalled for mandatory administrative processing." According to Wendy, what that really meant was additional security screening. It was almost laughable to think that the U.S. government considered frail eighty-year-old Sharif a security threat, but by now there was virtually no setback that would have surprised her.

Time was running out in the race to beat the new travel ban. In a last-ditch effort, Wendy emailed Senator Patty Murray's office, begging her to intervene with the embassy. Meanwhile, Maryan gave an interview to the local NBC affiliate, hoping to call attention to her family's plight. Neither attempt bore visible fruit. Every hour or so, Maryan would check the applicant portal on the U.S. Citizenship and Immigration Services' website to see if the status of Sharif's visa had changed. Wendy had warned her that administrative processing usually dragged on for months and even years, but something told her to keep checking. "I was checking every minute: *Is it ready?* I must have checked it five hundred times a day," she recalled. And then on the morning of March 15, the status suddenly changed. Sharif's visa was once again ready for pickup, less than twenty-four hours before the ban was scheduled to take effect.

Maryan raced to coordinate with her brother to get Sharif to the embassy immediately. They now knew for sure that Kaltuma's visa wouldn't be ready in time. Her father would have to go ahead without her, while they prayed that the courts would strike down the second ban as well. Maryan searched for flights that would get him out of Nairobi and into international airspace before the executive order went into force. There was a Delta flight through Amsterdam that left at 11:59 p.m. She gasped when she saw that it cost more than $1,800, but she went ahead and bought it anyway. She had talked it over with Wendy, and she knew there was still a chance that Sharif would be turned away at the border. Technically, Customs and Border Protection were supposed to honor visas that were issued prior to the March 16 deadline, but she knew that there had already been complications for Somalis arriving at Seattle's Sea-Tac Airport ahead of the ban. Maryan was rolling the dice, but after everything she had been through, she wasn't about to give up.

While Maryan scrambled to get her father on the plane, Wendy arranged to have a colleague look out for Sharif when he arrived in Seattle the next day. Attorneys had converged on international airports across the country to assist refugees and other foreign nationals targeted under the travel ban; they were camped out in arrivals halls and airport lounges from New York to Baltimore to Seattle. Wendy sent Sharif's information to airportlawyer.org, an app created by attorneys and technologists seeking to coordinate the haphazard response. She also emailed a lawyer named Diane, who she knew would be volunteering at Sea-Tac that day. If anything went wrong, Diane would be ready to intervene and try to prevent Sharif from being deported.

Maryan checked in with Wendy periodically throughout the day on the 16th. After a two-hour layover at Sea-Tac, Sharif had been scheduled to continue on to Pasco, where Maryan planned to pick him up at 4:21 p.m. But around 1 p.m. she heard from Wendy that he had fallen ill on the flight and been taken off the plane in Seattle on a stretcher, apparently because of dehydration. Customs and Border Protection had agreed to defer clearance so that he could be rushed to the hospital. But Maryan was stuck watching her children, so she couldn't meet him and help with the paperwork. Instead, a friend of hers named Aden agreed to fly to Sea-Tac, get Sharif officially stamped into the country, and pick up his green card. That night, Maryan spoke to her father on the phone for the first time since he landed on U.S. soil. The doctors had diagnosed him with pneumonia, he said, so they would have to keep him overnight. But he sounded overjoyed to be there. The hospital food was delicious, he reported, and for the first time in his life, people were falling over themselves to help him.

It would be another five months before Kaltuma joined them in the United States. Hours before Sharif had boarded his flight, a district court judge in Hawaii had blocked elements of the second travel ban from going into effect, prolonging the window in which she could conceivably get through. But the DNA tests took a few more months to complete, during which time she and Asad remained stuck in Eastleigh. In August, her visa was finally approved, a little more than a month before Trump signed a third iteration of his travel ban and slammed the door shut once again. Twenty-six years after they had fled Somalia, and thirteen years after they had been promised safe haven in America, both of her parents were finally reunited with Maryan in the United States. Asad and Ibrahim, and their two younger siblings, now thirteen and seventeen, had been left behind.

Book Two

JOURNEYS

VII

IN THE FOOTSTEPS OF AL-SHABAB

Nairobi, Kenya-Mogadishu, Somalia, September 2017

Sharif would have preferred a television, but he settled for hours of idle conversation with his son. In the months they had lived in Eastleigh waiting for his visa, he and Asad had spent more time together than they had in many years. Asad would sit on a chair, and Sharif would recline on a mattress on the floor, his knobby knees folded beneath him like a pair of collapsible tent poles. Five times a day at even intervals, he would pitch himself up and prepare to pray—either at a nearby mosque or on a woven prayer rug he unfurled on the floor. In the hours in between prayer sessions, as the muffled sounds of traffic filtered up from the street, he told stories of the country he had been forced to leave behind.

Sharif was born in 1937, twenty-three years before Somalia

gained independence. Back then the only people concerned with national borders had been the British and Italians. Like most nomadic Somalis, he considered much of what is now northeastern Kenya and eastern Ethiopia his domain. Even as the Europeans drew and redrew their largely theoretical boundaries, he zigzagged across them with his herds of camels and goats. Born in Luuq, a small settlement in southwestern Somalia that is almost completely encircled by an O-shaped meander in the Jubba River, he returned there frequently throughout his life. As a pastoralist, he didn't own land in the way the Europeans understood land ownership, but he would plant crops in the rich soil along the riverbank in one season and come back to harvest them the next.

His view of the Greater Somali region fit with his view of the independence movements that swept Africa when he was in his early twenties. He saw them as interconnected, united by a shared African identity that transcended European-style nationalism. He listened, rapt, to the radio as colonial regimes collapsed across the continent, and he can still recall the words to liberation songs from Djibouti to Mozambique. But his optimism faded after Somalia's second president, Abdirashid Shermarke, was assassinated and Siad Barre took power in 1969.

Tensions soon flared with neighboring Ethiopia, and Sharif was conscripted into the army, which in the mid 1970s began a massive Soviet-backed military buildup that culminated in an ill-fated invasion of Ethiopia. Thousands died on both sides, but Sharif's regiment was spared, remaining garrisoned in Mogadishu. Somalia lost the war after the Soviets switched sides and threw their support behind Ethiopia's Marxist-Leninist regime. Afterward, Sharif returned to the region around Luuq, settling at first in a camp for displaced people but intending to make a more permanent home. There he met a beautiful smooth-skinned woman named Kaltuma, who had grown up in Ethiopia and fled to Somalia in the early 1970s, after a series of clashes between separatists and the government. The two of them got married and moved out of the camp, eventually building a farm and a quiet life for themselves near the banks of the river. But things were becoming precarious for Sharif's clan, the Ashraf, which practiced a mystical form of Islam and claimed to be descended from the Prophet Mohammed. As Barre began to lose his grip on power, he pitted the more powerful clans against each other so they couldn't unite against his rule. The Ashraf were not a powerful clan, but historically they had played an important role mediating between them— allied to none but protected by all. As clan affiliation became essential for security, however, the Ashraf's independence became a liability. "There was nowhere in Somalia that belonged to us," Sharif recalled. "We used to live at peace with every clan, but over time it became unsafe. If bad things happened to other clans, bad things happened to us, too."

Sharif felt a deep attachment to Luuq, and the stories he told were full of vivid details—of the lush foliage that clung to the riverbanks, of the sturdy trees that reached high into a typically cloudless sky. But that was before the war, which began when Barre's regime collapsed in 1991 and sent Sharif's family into exile for more than a quarter century. He had been back to his hometown only once in the intervening years, in 2015, when his sister had fallen ill. He had crossed back into Somalia from Dadaab, following a route well worn by smugglers and black-market traders. What he had found devastated him: a city torn apart by years of fighting and occupied by Ethiopian troops. "The place looked like a place where foreigners came to fight," he told Asad one day as they sat in the darkened hotel room. If it had been Somalis doing the fighting, Sharif explained, they would have felt ashamed of the level of destruction. "That place . . . ," he said, trailing off. "There's no hope for that place."

. . .

For years Asad had been gathering what he thought of as little slivers of Somalia. Some of them came from the stories relayed by friends and family. Others came from books by African scholars, many of them written in the heady post-independence period. One sliver he was reminded of as he listened to his father was the tale of Hawa Tako, a Somali freedom fighter who was killed during violent anti-imperial protests in 1948 and who later became a focus of Barre's nationalist hagiography. A Joan of Arc–like figure, Tako appears on Somalia's now worthless 100-shilling note, rifle and shovel held aloft and a baby at her breast. Her likeness also looms over a traffic circle near the old National Theater in Mogadishu, part of a monument built by Barre in 1972.

Sharif was eleven when Tako was killed, either by an Italian officer's bullet or, as the Somali novelist Nuruddin Farah has written, by a poisoned arrow shot by a colonial sympathizer. By the time Barre erected the statue of her twenty-five years later, Sharif had already grown cynical about Somalia's post-independence leaders. But hearing him say that he had lost all hope in his country was difficult for Asad to accept. Ever since he could remember, he had longed to go to Somalia, to trade the slivers collected over the years for fully formed memories of his own.

After his parents departed for the United States, the idea of a journey began to take shape. The previous nine months shepherding his parents' visa applications had been stressful, an endless slog of appointments and interviews and requests for documentation. Each time a new piece of evidence had been required, it had been up to him to produce it: birth certificates, a marriage license, a security clearance from the Kenyan government. Since neither of his parents had a *kitambulisho*, both of them had to submit photographs and fingerprints to the same predatory police that he was afraid might deport them. Asad had spent weeks hanging around the notorious Criminal Investigations Department, befriending officers and support staff before he found the right person to bribe. Now that both of his parents were safe in America, it felt like a tremendous weight had been lifted. If there was ever a time to follow in their footsteps—to see for himself what Somalia had become—it was now that they were finally gone.

But for the first time in a long time, there was also a reason to stay. For months after he received the crushing email from David Ongwae, he had scarcely been able to open a book. Depressed and defeated, he had convinced himself that Ongwae was right: that he wasn't as clever or as wise as he thought. But after a long hiatus in which he had written almost nothing, he had started to ease back into it. All he had ever wanted was to be a writer, and as his darkest thoughts receded, he began to indulge that possibility again. Even if he remained trapped in Dadaab for the rest of his life, he told himself, his prose could still reach people around the world. With little else to do, he imposed a rigorous schedule on himself, writing one article per week and submitting it to the *New York Times,* which he considered, with the exception of the *New Yorker,* the pinnacle of journalism.

By the time an editor finally wrote him back, he had submitted more than forty articles without receiving a reply. The editor rejected his pitch, but to Asad's surprise, he invited him to submit other article ideas. After some back-and-forth, they agreed that Asad would write an essay about his sister's return to Dadaab and about the Kenyan government's threats to close the camp. "As ever, we do not know what will happen to us," he wrote in an article that appeared under the headline "Waiting for Maryan" in the November 20, 2016, issue of the *New York Times Magazine*.

The article provided a much-needed boost, erasing some of the doubts that had accumulated over the previous year and providing an entrée to reconnect with the journalists he had sought out years earlier, at the *Daily Nation* and at the journal *Sahan*. Suddenly, he was a minor celebrity in Somali intellectual circles, the self-taught refugee writer who had somehow gotten the attention of the *New York Times*. Never mind that he still wasn't allowed to work, or that the *Times* had to wire payment to his sister because he didn't have a bank account— the article put him on the map, and it began to open doors that he had previously thought were closed.

While he was caring for his parents in Eastleigh, he had grown close to two writers in particular. One was Abdi Latif Dahir, a handsome, doe-eyed journalist with short hair and tortoise-shell glasses who had studied at Columbia before joining the business website *Quartz* in Nairobi. (Later, he would become the *New York Times*'s East Africa correspondent.) The other was Abdinasir Amin, a soft-spoken public health PhD who worked on malaria prevention by day and wrote about "matters bookish," as he put it, by night. All three of them wrote for *Sahan*, which at the time was dedicated mainly to the Somali literary scene. The two Abdis lent Asad books, as well as their log-in credentials to various online subscriptions. They also encouraged him to enroll in the journalism program at United States International University Africa, a private four-year college in Nairobi where Abdi Latif had gone before Columbia. A degree wouldn't fix the problem of his immigration status, or give him the right to work when he graduated, but it might pave the way to graduate school in the United States, as it had for Abdi Latif.

Asad's grades on the national high school exam hadn't been good enough for the WUSC, but they qualified him to enroll at most Kenyan universities, provided he could afford the tuition. Asad had applied to the only other scholarship available to refugees, a German-funded program called the Albert Einstein German Academic Refugee Initiative, but he hadn't been selected for that one either. The Abdis offered to pay his tuition at USIU, agreeing to take turns covering the more than $1,200 in fees each year. It was an extraordinary act of generosity, one that Asad wasn't sure how to adequately respond to. He had never been good at accepting gifts. It was harder than you would think, being the beneficiary of other people's kindness. What he really wanted was to be able to support himself. But knowing that was impossible, he accepted the Abdis' offer.

By the time his mother finally left for the United States in August, Asad had finished his first semester at USIU, where he had received all A's and B's. But even as he selected his second-semester classes, he couldn't stop thinking about what his father had said. He needed to see Somalia with his own eyes, to decide for himself whether it was hopeless. More than anything, he needed Sharif to be wrong. Coming to Nairobi had been exhilarating, a welcome break from the monotony of Dadaab. But his tangles with the Kenyan bureaucracy had left him more convinced than ever that he would never be fully welcome there. It wasn't that he wanted to return permanently to Somalia. That would be folly, he knew. Rather, he needed to know there was somewhere on earth where he belonged. "Kenya will never accept me, I realized. I will always just be a refugee," he said. "I wanted not to be a refugee."

. . .

The truck rolled out of Dadaab at dusk. It was loaded high with sacks of beans, which were held in place with heavy tires, their deep treads offering grubby hand-holds to the passengers perched on top. Asad hadn't told anyone where he was going, not his family and not the Abdis. They would have tried to talk him out of what he knew deep down was a foolish journey. Instead, he had called Bekar, who had taken the same route two years before, after his parents had returned to Somalia.

The two of them sat next to each other beneath a star-sprinkled sky. Over the steady growl of the engine, they could hear the malevolent laughter of hyenas. Getting across the border wouldn't be difficult. People and goods moved from northeastern Kenya into Somalia on a daily basis, shunning formal immigration procedures just as Sharif had done in his pastoralist days. The only difference was that Kenyan security forces now patrolled the frontier, extracting informal taxes at gunpoint and occasionally disappearing people.

On the Somali side of the border, it was al-Shabab who did the taxing and the killing. Travelers could generally pass safely through the group's stronghold, so long as they followed the rules: At the first checkpoint, you filled out a customs form, just like you would if you were entering any other country. Then you paid a standard levy, based on the amount of cargo you were carrying. Smartphones—with their access to potentially corrupting information and entertainment—were prohibited, as were alcohol, drugs, and tobacco. Violate any of these rules, and you might have to pay with your life.

There were other risks as well. Al-Shabab was known to kidnap young men and force them to join their insurgency against the Somali government. The group's fighters, many of them just boys, also tended to mete out their version of justice on the spot, meaning that a suspected spy or journalist might face summary execution based on the hunch of a twelve-year-old. But in general, the rules were more predictable than under the corrupt Somali government, to the point that many businessmen preferred the roads controlled by al-Shabab.

It was morning when they entered Somalia. There was no official border crossing, nothing to denote the end of Kenyan sovereignty. It was just the same stubby trees growing under the same blue sky. They bumped along for another few hours before reaching their first village. It seemed mostly abandoned and eerily quiet. They stopped next to a black flag that would have typically signaled an al-Shabab checkpoint, but when no one appeared they continued on. They passed through several more abandoned villages before they reached the town of Waraha Dhoobleey, which was larger than the previous settlements and livelier. It was there that they met their first al-Shabab fighter, a boy of seventeen or eighteen who carried no weapon and wore no uniform. Asad watched as the driver filled out the customs form and paid the tax: $230 for the truck, its cargo, and twelve passengers.

The pattern repeated itself as they moved from village to village, and Asad was struck by the uniformity of the process. There might have been terror in al-Shabab's domain, but there was order as well, and that was more than could be said of the rest of the country, he knew. If people here talked about al-Shabab, they were supportive of its cause. No one he met expressed support for the Somali government. No one had received a government service of any kind.

But not everyone followed the rules, at least not all the time. On the road in between settlements, the passengers smoked cigarettes and listened to music on their phones. When they were approaching the next settlement, the driver would signal, the banned activities would cease, and the tobacco and phones would be stashed out of sight. On the afternoon of the third day, the truck passed a young man walking alone on the desert road. He waved the driver down and hitched a ride, hauling himself up onto the sacks of beans with the other passengers. Asad didn't think much of the man until that evening, when they were pulling into Buaale, an expansive settlement of low concrete structures with painted metal roofs. Like Luuq, which lies roughly 200 miles to the north, Buaale sits on the banks of the winding Jubba River, its tall trees and dense foliage drawing strength from the murky reddish-brown water. In anticipation of a checkpoint, everyone hid their phones and tossed their cigarettes. Asad slipped a notebook he had been journaling in to the driver, who concealed it in the cabin of the truck. When they came to a stop outside a dilapidated white structure pocked with bullet holes, they were greeted by a phalanx of men in army fatigues. Unlike the al-Shabab fighters they had encountered previously, these men carried rifles and were draped in heavy belts of ammunition. And to Asad's horror, they offered a friendly greeting to the traveler they had picked up earlier in the day. "He's one of them and he knows our secrets," Asad thought to himself, a feeling of dread suddenly coming over him.

The armed men separated the passengers by sex. Then they searched everyone's bags, but patted only the men down. If they found his notebook, Asad figured that would be the end for him. Already, he had attracted additional scrutiny at previous checkpoints. In a land with no healthcare, his eyeglasses marked him as a foreigner and a potential spy. Add a pen and paper to that equation, and he was a dead man. And it wouldn't be a pleasant death, either, since al-Shabab was known to occasionally saw its victims' heads off while they were still alive. "No one in your family even knows where you are," he thought to himself. "You're just going to disappear."

One of the men traveling with them hadn't cut his hair short in the manner decreed by the extremist group. The fighters singled him out and threatened to kill him. Then they took a razor blade and sheared a sponge-sized strip of hair out of his scalp. Another man was found with a cell phone. "You will either destroy it, or you will leave this world," one of the al-Shabab fighters said, handing him a hammer. The man obediently smashed the device, sending shards of metal and plastic skittering across the ground. The militants found nothing in Asad's or Bekar's luggage, but it wasn't until the last passenger had been searched and allowed back on the truck that he breathed a sigh of relief. The al-Shabab member they had unwittingly picked up by the side of the road hadn't revealed their secret, and his colleagues hadn't searched the truck.

. . .

They spent the night in Buaale, rising at dawn with the call to prayer. All of the other passengers had gotten off in town, so it was just Bekar and Asad on top of the sacks when the truck pulled back onto the road. In the cab down below were the driver, Adan, and two men in his employ. As soon as they left the river basin, the landscape grew arid and dusty again. There were still pockets of trees and scrub, but the ground was sandy and parched. Here and there gravelly washes had swallowed whole chunks of the road, the work of long-forgotten floods. No one maintained the roads in al-Shabab country, so they had a way of sprouting new arteries around fallen trees or other obstacles. Sometimes Bekar wasn't sure they were on a road at all. Maybe they were simply following the tire tracks of trucks that had carved their own paths through the wilderness.

Bekar had his own reasons for returning to Somalia. After Asad had left Dadaab to finish high school in Kiisi, he had toiled on in Room 101 for another six months. When regular classes at Ifo Secondary still hadn't resumed, he took a bus to Garissa and talked his way into a boarding school there, convincing the headmaster to waive the fees. Soon after, his family decided to return to Somalia. His grandmother, who had stayed behind in Mogadishu when the rest of the family fled, had fallen ill, and his mother felt she needed to care for her. Bekar remained alone in Kenya to finish high school, scoring a B+ on the national exam in 2014 that he thought would qualify him for the WUSC. But his application was rejected that year and the next; the competition for the scholarship had grown stiffer over the years, and a high grade was no longer a guarantee of a place. Finally, he applied for the same Albert Einstein German Academic Refugee Initiative that Asad had sought unsuccessfully. The scholarship covered tuition at Kenyan universities and was regarded as a kind of consolation prize. It wasn't a ticket to a new life in Canada, or even a path to gainful employment in Kenya, but it was something to do for the next four years.

Bekar won the scholarship and enrolled in a health sciences program at Moi University in Eldoret, a highland city of wide avenues and towering evergreens in the heart of the Rift Valley. By then it had been three years since he had seen his family, and Raaliyo, his late father's second wife, had passed away. Without a passport, the only way to visit them was to make the perilous weeklong journey through al-Shabab territory. As a child, he had lived under the Islamic Courts Union, whose militant youth wing later morphed into al-Shabab. But what he saw in the southern Somali villages he passed through was something else entirely. He was shocked by the discipline of the insurgents, and by the degree to which they had subdued the local population. Unlike the Somali and Kenyan governments, al-Shabab didn't appear to be corrupt. If its members found money in your pocket, they always left it alone. At the same time, they were harsh and fanatical. "If you have a phone with a memory card, you will eat that memory, for sure," he said. "You either follow their rules or you die. No other options."

Now, a little more than two years later, he was making the same trip to see his family again—this time with Asad. Six or seven hours after they left Buaale, when the sun was still high in the sky, the truck swerved suddenly and skidded to a halt. A moment later, Adan was shouting for them to come down and help. They had slid almost entirely off the road, leaving the wheels sunk up to their axels in the loose, silty earth. When Adan stepped on the gas, the submerged tires just spat up dirt and sucked the undercarriage closer to the ground.

For the next few hours, the five of them worked together to unload the heavy sacks of beans onto the ground. With a lightened load, Adan hoped they could maneuver the truck back onto the road. But by sundown they were all exhausted and the vehicle still wouldn't budge. Bekar shinnied up to the top of a tree looking for signs of civilization, but there was nothing but dry brush and withered trees for as far as the eye could see. They were stranded in the wilderness, at least half a day's drive from the nearest village. That night they slept by the side of the road, praying that another vehicle would happen upon them and offer assistance. But Bekar wasn't feeling hopeful; not a single soul had passed them all day.

They had left Buaale with four yellow jerry cans filled with water. By the next morning, they were down to two. When Asad went to drink from one of the cans, Adan motioned for him to stop. That was his water, Adan said, his expression growing unexpectedly hard. He didn't know how much longer it would have to last. "From now on, you're not going to touch it." Bekar suddenly realized that the driver was prepared to let the two of them die if it meant prolonging his own life for another few hours. He wondered if he and Asad could overpower Adan if it came to that.

By noon, Bekar had begun to feel dizzy and dehydrated.

He lay down in the shade of a tree and tried to sleep for a while. When he woke up, it was late afternoon. He felt short of breath now and his vision was blurry. For the second time in two days, he thought, "This is the end of your life." But just as the sun was beginning to set, he heard Asad shouting excitedly. A beat-up minibus was approaching from the direction of Buaale, and strapped to the roof he could see a row of yellow jerry cans.

· · ·

Asad and Bekar left Adan and his men to dig their truck out of the sand, climbing aboard the minibus after drinking appreciatively from their rescuers' water supply (and watching somewhat disapprovingly as Adan refilled his jerry cans as well). Two days later, the bus reached the outskirts of Afgooye, roughly fifteen miles west of Mogadishu. A verdant agricultural enclave that was once a favorite holiday destination of the moneyed elite, Afgooye was now a city of castaways. "The country's capital of the displaced," was how one newspaper reporter described it in 2010, when the UN estimated that more than 400,000 uprooted Somalis were living in temporary shelters along the narrow corridor that runs from Afgooye to the capital. The town was also the beginning of the Somali government's sphere of influence, a fact announced by the presence of Burundian peacekeepers—part of the African Union mission fighting al-Shabab—who patrolled the streets in pickup trucks and space-age armored vehicles. There were also "scrawny

Somali boys with guns roaming the streets," Asad would write later in an account of his journey published by the *New York Times*. "I was told they were the government."

Life in government-controlled Somalia was very different than in the regions ruled by al-Shabab. There were more shops and restaurants and hotels—evidence of a booming wartime economy that had clearly enriched some at the expense of many. People walked down the street blaring music from their phones, and lounged in open-air cafés, where they chewed *miraa* and watched soccer and dubbed Bollywood soaps. But the freedom enjoyed by people here seemed as much a product of anarchy as of purposeful government policy. Armed men were ubiquitous in the capital. Some wore the green uniforms of the ragtag Somali National Army. Others wore civilian clothes, accessorized with belts of ammunition and rocket-propelled grenades. The unspoken rule of the road was that the most heavily armed vehicle had the right of way.

The first dead bodies he saw were a few blocks from the presidential palace, a heavily fortified art deco mansion that overlooks a cascade of bulbous neem trees and painted metal roofs sloping down to the pale blue of the Indian Ocean. He and Bekar had just stepped out of the blinding white midday sun into the cool shade of a mosque, when they heard what sounded like an explosion outside. A car bomb had ripped through a busy nearby intersection, leaving a gruesome scene of severed limbs and smoldering metal scrap. To Asad, the most dispiriting thing was how people reacted. They seemed casual, almost unfazed. It was as if it was a "normal thing," he recalled. "It happens so often that people don't think it's a big thing." A few days later a second explosion rocked the capital, claiming half a dozen lives.

This normalization of violence was everywhere on display, in the private security and blast-proof HESCO barriers that guarded anything of value, in the callousness of patrolling African Union peacekeepers who ran civilians off the road in their armored vehicles, in the daily destruction of life and property that registered as little more than background noise. New luxury hotels and gated communities had sprouted up here and there, financed by speculative investors with healthy appetites for risk. But much of the city was still a living monument to the war. Crumbling limestone villas lined the old Italian harbor, their glassless windows staring vacantly out at bobbing fishing boats like empty eye sockets. Just a few blocks inland, through a maze of bullet-scarred buildings, the ruined Mogadishu Cathedral spilled its stony guts into the street. Not far from there, in the direction of the Central Hotel, where two years prior al-Shabab had slaughtered at least eleven people, a beleaguered Hawa Tako still bore witness to the city's suffering from her chipped pedestal.

. . .

Returning to Kenya the same way he had come, through the vast swath of southern Somalia that had slipped beyond the government's control, Asad couldn't escape feeling that his father had been right. "The whole trip was just a confirmation of what he said," he recalled. "I genuinely came to the same conclusion." Nothing remained of the romanticized Somalia of the 1960s. In its place, he found a country that was carved into two separate fiefdoms, one offering freedom and the other, security. As long as Somalis were forced to choose between the two, he thought, there was little hope for the future.

It was a painful realization, but one that in some ways made it easier to resume the precarious life of a refugee in Kenya. With the fate of Dadaab still uncertain, at least he knew he had to move his two younger siblings to Nairobi with him rather than to Somalia. So with the help of the Abdis and Maryan, he arranged for them to be smuggled out of the camp. The three of them moved into a cramped one-bedroom in Eastleigh, not far from the hotel where he and his parents had stayed. It was a stop-gap measure, but if he was being honest, his entire life had been a sequence of stop-gap measures. With so many crises demanding his attention all at once, long-term planning simply wasn't an option.

Asad found new schools for both of his siblings, religious ones that were willing to accept them without papers. He also returned to USIU for a second semester, enrolling in courses in journalism and political science. After being in Somalia, it felt strange to have theoretical discussions about politics and war—"these people have no idea," he thought to himself in class discussions. But he did his best to put his personal feelings aside and apply himself.

One day he was outside the auditorium on campus when he got a call from a number he didn't recognize. It was a woman named Sue who said she helped run a scholarship for Kenyan students. She had read his article in the *New York Times,* she explained, and she wanted to know if he was interested in applying. He would probably have to go back and repeat his final year of high school, she said, rather apologetically. But after that he would have a chance to go to England for university. Cambridge, Manchester, Bristol—Sue said her scholarship students had attended all of these. It all sounded pretty farfetched to Asad. Who was this woman and why did she want to give him a scholarship? And why was she asking him to drop out of university and go back to high school? Didn't she know that was a step backward? But Sue sounded positive, excited even, and at the end of the call he heard himself agreeing to meet in person. "I might as well," he thought. "What do I have to lose?"

VIII

A BEACON OF HOPE

Nairobi, Kenya, October 2017

B ehind a plain white door on the second floor of Nyaku House, a nondescript office complex in Nairobi's Hurlingham neighborhood known mainly to the gamblers who frequented the smoke-filled Finix Casino on the ground floor, Dr. Susan Kiragu was preparing for her first meeting of the day. It was mid-October, and outside in the sun the purple jacarandas were blooming. Inside it was dark and cool, and the barren walls gave the office an almost clinical feel. Dr. Sue placed a notepad and a book of IQ tests on the black boardroom table, then glanced at the clock behind her desk: a minute or two to 10 a.m. She was tired and a little frazzled. Two days before, thieves had attacked and robbed her on her way home from work. A white bandage on the right side of her head covered an inch-long gash she had sustained during the ordeal. Not one to let little inconveniences like that get in the way of work, she was back in the office to interview a young man she hoped would make a fine Beacon Scholar.

Dr. Sue had been working for the small privately endowed scholarship since 2014. Together with the scholarship's founders and main benefactors, a British-educated couple named Ajay and Antonia Sood, she helped to identify promising Kenyan students with leadership potential as well as financial need. Many of them went on to top British universities, including Cambridge and the London School of Economics. Some attended elite preparatory schools in Nairobi, before going abroad to university. A lifelong educator who was always on the lookout for promising youngsters, she had caught wind of a refugee who had somehow managed to publish an article in the *New York Times*. He hadn't been a stellar student, she had heard, but when she googled his name and read some of his writing, it was clear he had a way with words.

Before long there was a knock at the door. In padded a tall, gangly young man wearing a backpack and slim-fitting blue jeans. He smiled broadly and peered down at her through rectangular eyeglasses. But instead of a handshake, she felt her arms open reflexively and they embraced as if they were old friends. Almost immediately, she could sense that Asad was unlike any of the dozens of talented students who had gone through the Beacon Scholarship program over the years. Despite his awkward appearance, he exuded a quiet confidence that made him seem much older than his twenty-one years. And when she ran him through the various quizzes and tests that made up her academic evaluation, his dry and sometimes caustic answers caught her off guard.

"What goes up and down and has buttons?" was one of the questions she read from her IQ test booklet that day. Asad looked at her quizzically and shrugged.

"I don't know, a plane?"

The answer, she explained, was an elevator, which caused him to swear loudly and protest that he had only ever seen one of those once, a week ago at a mall called Yaya Center. In Dadaab, there had been no multistory buildings, let alone elevators to climb them.

But Asad was funny and warm and seemed to want to talk endlessly about novels, many of which Dr. Sue had never read. She had asked a current Beacon Scholar, a girl attending an American international school in Nairobi, to join them after an hour so she could observe him in a social setting. In her experience, the most severely disadvantaged students often struggled to connect with their more affluent peers. It was as if poverty had eroded their self-worth. But the two of them hit it off at once. Soon they were jabbering away about Steinbeck, Margaret Atwood, and a new television series called *The Handmaid's Tale* that was based on Atwood's novel of the same name.

The IQ test had been a disaster—"below the standard we usually expect of a Beacon Scholar," was the diplomatic assessment Dr. Sue would offer later—but there was no longer any doubt in her mind about whether Asad was deserving of a scholarship. The young man had some catching up to do for sure, so he would need to complete a one-year foundational program at a prep school in Nairobi before applying to university. But with a C+ on the national exam, no comprehensive school reports, and no standardized test scores, the challenge would be getting him in.

. . .

Dr. Sue had a habit of adopting strays. Round and ebullient, with short hair and sparkling almond-shaped eyes, she had spent nearly a decade since finishing her PhD at Cambridge bouncing around various academic, educational, and development-related jobs. In all of them she found herself growing emotionally attached to those she was supposed to study or serve from a distance, unable to adopt the kind of objective, dispassionate approach common among her colleagues. From 2009 to 2013, she helped run a longitudinal study of female primary school students in sixteen poor school districts in Kenya. The aim was to better understand the factors that kept girls in school "against the odds." But unlike her older, British colleagues from Cambridge's Center for Commonwealth Education who treated it as a purely academic exercise, she took it upon herself to remove some of the educational impediments they identified. Lack of bras and sanitary pads seemed to be keeping girls out of the classroom, so she packed suitcases full of them in Britain and dragged them with her to Kenya. Often, she would bring only one change of clothes for herself.

Over the course of the study, many of the girls dropped out. Of the original eighty-nine students, only thirty-three made it to graduation, and of those only eleven passed. Dr. Sue paid out of her own pocket for five of them to go to high school, and helped raise money for the others. Some of her Cambridge colleagues chipped in, but they seemed perplexed as to why their Kenyan colleague was so attached. "Everyone at Cambridge was like, 'Okay, you are going beyond academia,'" she recalled. "All that was expected of me was to publish."

Eventually, she left academia for the nonprofit world, managing research programs in Tanzania, Ghana, and Zimbabwe for the Campaign for Female Education, or Camfed. The work was more fulfilling than academic research, but she still had a nagging feeling that she could be doing more. At one point, she was in Tanzania checking up on one of Camfed's projects when it hit her that they were only investing about $10 per girl every year. "Oh my God, we can do better," she thought to herself.

So she quit and started her own organization, Children in Freedom, which offered more generous scholarships as well as mentorship to underprivileged students, mainly in marginalized parts of Kenya. At the same time, she began advising Ajay and Antonia on the Beacon Scholarship, and eventually she took over as the program's regional coordinator in East

Africa. In some ways, the Beacon's philosophy was the opposite of Camfed's. Instead of helping a large number of students a little bit, the Beacon made a huge investment in a small number of children in the hopes that their success would have ripple effects.

Asad's potential to lift up others was obvious. His writing focused on society's most vulnerable—refugees, women, social outcasts of various sorts—and took a rhetorical sledgehammer to the systemic injustices he observed. Barred from even the most basic forms of civic participation, he had figured out that writing was "what he could use to help others," Dr. Sue recalled. "You could see his life revolving around literature and using it as a tool, not only to tell his story, but as a political thing to change lives."

The trouble was that not everyone in the rarified world of private secondary education in Nairobi was interested in thinking hard about issues like displacement, much less having an actual refugee on campus. Many of the top boarding schools in Kenya were founded, consciously or not, on the model of Eton, that bastion of British privilege that spawned the fictional icons Bertie Wooster and James Bond, not to mention twenty actual prime ministers. At the Brookhouse School, where Dr. Sue hoped Asad could enroll for his postgraduate year, fees for boarding students exceeded $20,000 per year—this in a country where nearly half of households earn less than $100 a month. The school offered a handful of scholarships, but the vast majority of students paid full tuition, ensuring they hailed from the country's most privileged class.

Brookhouse was a formal partner of the Beacon, but Dr. Sue was already encountering resistance. After their initial interview, Asad had gone for a separate meeting with Eric Mulindi, head of secondary education at Brookhouse, as well as several members of his staff, including an acquaintance of Dr. Sue's named Joyce Gacheru. From what Dr. Sue heard afterward, the meeting had gone well. Asad had refrained from swearing, and generally impressed the administrators, especially Mr. Mulindi, as the headmaster was known on campus. Joyce had even called to say she was optimistic: "He's got what it takes and we'll try our best to take him onboard," she said.

But then the school counselor in charge of scholarship students called. When Dr. Sue had met her on previous occasions, the counselor had always seemed thoughtful and kind. But over the phone she sounded annoyed, even a tad upset. She hadn't attended the interview with Asad, but she didn't think he would "fit into Brookhouse," she said. Besides, at twenty-one he would be a year or two older than most of the students in the postgraduate course, called the International Foundation Year, or IFY. "He is overage, and we don't take refugees," Dr. Sue recalled her saying.

Dr. Sue was disappointed to hear that sentiment expressed by a member of the Brookhouse faculty, but not entirely surprised. She had spent much of her life battling discrimination, whether by white Westerners against Africans or by Africans of one stripe against another. She pleaded with the counselor to reconsider, asking her to meet Asad in person and to arrange a second interview with John O'Connor, the school's director, whose support she thought might be able to outweigh any concerns about Asad's age. But when she hung up, she wasn't feeling hopeful.

• • •

There seemed no end to the number of hoops Asad was supposed to jump through. In addition to the IQ and leadership tests, the observed social interactions, and the interviews, there were two sets of application forms. One for Brookhouse, which was five pages long, and another for the Beacon, which was fourteen pages. Asad was still skeptical of the whole idea, but after his meetings with Dr. Sue and Mr. Mulindi, he had agreed to at least fill out the forms. He didn't have a laptop, though, so he settled into a cyber café in Eastleigh to fill them out. He didn't get far before he encountered his first problem.

In the very first section of the Brookhouse application, immediately following the field where he typed his name, the form asked for his mailing address. Unsure of what to write, since he had never received anything by post, he left it blank and moved on to the next field: nationality. That one also presented a quandary, since neither his country of birth nor his parents' countries of birth claimed him as a citizen. He typed "refugee" and moved on to the next question: What nation's passport do you travel on? That one he skipped as well, along with the next two, which asked for his passport number and its date of expiry. The next field said religion—finally, something he could answer. He typed "Muslim" and continued scrolling down.

But the pages that followed contained more unanswerable questions. His parents' employers and business addresses, for instance. (Neither of them had ever held a formal job.) There was also a section for students with special needs, which a parent or guardian was supposed to fill out, asking if he had any learning disabilities or had ever received any special assistance. Neither of his parents were literate or spoke English for that matter, so he decided to shelve that section for now as well.

Dr. Sue had called to ask how he was getting on with the application, urging him to fill it out quickly so she could discuss it with Ajay and Antonia. Asad had taken an immediate liking to Dr. Sue. She struck him as earnest and bighearted, one of those rare, guileless souls who couldn't help but see the best in others. And for whatever reason, she seemed to believe in him, something he wasn't sure he could say about himself. She had made it clear that Brookhouse's admissions process was separate from the Beacon's, but winning over Ajay and Antonia was the first hurdle he had to clear. Doing so would require yet another interview, this one with the couple over Skype.

Asad wasn't sure what to expect. He looked Ajay and Antonia up online, as he had done with Dr. Sue and Mr. Mulindi prior to meeting them. He learned that Ajay, who was of Indian descent, had been born in Kisumu, Kenya's third-largest city, and attended the prestigious Pembroke House School. He had been elected the head boy there, before going off to Canada to study law and commerce. Later, he obtained an MBA at London Business School, worked for American Express, and founded a successful publishing company with Antonia. Antonia, who was blonde and British, had also received an MBA at London Business School. Before that she had worked at the Ministry of Defense and in development across sub-Saharan Africa. Together they had founded the Beacon Scholarship in 2008, and from what Dr. Sue and others told him, they had poured a substantial sum of their own money into it, helping to educate dozens of young Kenyans.

In the interview, Ajay took the lead. Bearded and swarthy, with an expansive bald pate that took up much of the computer screen, he struck Asad as cold and businesslike. Unlike Dr. Sue, who had been at pains to make him feel comfortable, Ajay bordered on brusque. He gave Asad a chance to speak about his writing and academic interests, but he soon embarked on a line of questioning that put Asad on the defensive. "I can see that you are from a poor family, and you didn't have the upbringing that these rich kids did," Asad remembered him saying. Ajay wanted to know if he would be able to adjust. More to the point, he wanted to know how he would respond to taunting and abuse from wealthier boys. He seemed concerned that Asad might try to fight them.

The questions struck Asad as absurd. Did Ajay really think that all poor people had bad manners? That they had no respect for others and were more prone to violence? He could feel the indignation rising in his chest, but tamped it down out of sight. This wasn't the time to confront Ajay about the troubling assumptions that seemed to lie beneath his questions. Instead, he offered what he hoped was a reassuring response: "We were poor, but we weren't taught to fight each other." Inside he thought, *What the fuck?*

...

The decision to admit Asad was a contentious one. The counselor in charge of scholarships wasn't the only person at Brookhouse who thought he was a bad idea. Divya Chaudry, or Mrs. Chaudry, who taught biology and led the yearlong IFY program to which he was applying, had reservations as well. A strict disciplinarian who had done her undergraduate studies in the United Kingdom, she didn't like the idea of accepting a student who lacked proper immigration papers. Other teachers involved in the process wondered aloud if he might be dangerous. "'You're taking a student who says he lives in Eastleigh,'" Mr. Mulindi, the headmaster, remembered one of his colleagues saying. "'How sure are you he's not part of a Somali terrorist group?'"

Mr. Mulindi thought that was outrageous, but he initially

shared his colleagues' concern about Asad's age. Quiet and plainspoken, with the patient air of an educator, the headmaster had thought first about the need to maintain a relatively sheltered environment for the youngest children on campus. But after he met with Asad and heard the remarkable lengths to which he had gone to get an education, he felt sure the young man wouldn't cause any trouble. He had reminded Asad that he would have to wear a uniform like all the other students, and submit to the round-the-clock supervision that was the norm at boarding school. Asad's reply—that he would do whatever it took to get an education—had struck him as honest and admirable. This was someone on a mission, and Mr. Mulindi wasn't about to stand in his way.

Dr. Sue's lobbying had also helped persuade him. She had been unwavering in her support for Asad, and when she and Ajay indicated that they planned to award him a Beacon Scholarship, any lingering doubts he had about the boy, whose application had a few too many blank spaces, faded away. Ajay had a reputation for being prickly, but the scholarship he and Antonia had built was well regarded. The boys and girls they supported were highly accomplished, and they went on to impressive institutions. If Dr. Sue and Ajay thought Asad was worthy of a Beacon Scholarship, that was reason enough to admit him.

But there was one more reason Mr. Mulindi was inclined to open the door for Asad. Unlike many of his colleagues who came from well-to-do families and had been educated abroad, Mr. Mulindi grew up poor in rural western Kenya. At his provincial primary school, students went barefoot, eating wild fruits and sugar cane for lunch. The high school he later attended in the town of Kakamega required pupils to wear shoes, so his father bought him his first pair. Worried they would be stolen and he wouldn't be allowed back in the classroom, he slept in them for days. It was a story he liked to tell at Brookhouse, where it was a rare student who had endured financial hardship. Many had no idea how most people lived in Kenya's impoverished hinterlands, let alone in its refugee camps. The country they saw consisted only of the leafy suburbs of the capital, its many upscale shopping malls, and the international airport from which they jetted off to holidays in Europe. Mr. Mulindi had always encouraged his students to venture outside this bubble of privilege. Forcing them to study alongside Asad would go some way toward puncturing it from within, an outcome he thought would benefit everyone.

Because of the unusual level of disagreement among the staff, Mr. Mulindi decided it would be wise to get Mr. O'Connor, the school's director, to issue the final verdict. But he also let it be known where he stood on the matter. In private, he told O'Connor how impressed he was by Asad's determination. He said he was especially moved by his ability to overcome setback after setback, whether it was a terrorist attack that disrupted his schooling or an article submission to the *New York Times* that went unanswered.

On the appointed day, Mr. Mulindi accompanied Asad to his meeting in Mr. O'Connor's office, on the second floor of the school's Spanish-style administration building. Asad was dressed in khaki trousers and a navy blazer that covered only about three-quarters of his rangy forearms—a getup that looked like it had been borrowed from a smaller student for the occasion. The two of them sat across from each other in front of Mr. O'Connor's thick wooden desk, and Mr. Mulindi tried his best to look reassuring. Asad seemed nervous, swallowing hard and getting the occasional word stuck in the back of his throat. But Mr. O'Connor appeared moved when he heard Asad describe his journey in his own words. By the end of the meeting, it was clear to everyone that Asad would have a place at Brookhouse. To Mr. Mulindi, he looked exhausted but pleased, like a boy who had just cleared the last hurdle on a long obstacle course.

IX

CULTURE SHOCK

Nairobi, Kenya, November 2017

Far from the honking, belching traffic that surges through Nairobi at all hours, and farther still from the heaving slums that house millions of impoverished Kenyans, sits the stately campus of the Brookhouse School. Its turreted castle-like buildings overlook fourteen pristine acres adjacent to a national park; peacocks and ostriches roam the carefully manicured grounds. The school's elegant Burudani Theater was the site of Kenya's first nationally televised presidential debate in 2013, and Margaret Kenyatta, the first lady, who endowed an eponymous scholarship there, could often be seen coming and going in a fleet of black Mercedes sedans.

On the second or third day of orientation, Asad was seated in the front row of a small auditorium packed with students dressed in russet blazers and university striped ties. The coordinator of the International Foundation Year program, the diminutive Mrs. Chaudry, was explaining how the course they were embarking on would prepare them to enter any one of roughly a dozen selective British universities in nine months' time. It was an accelerated postgraduate program, and the pace of instruction would be fast. The students would have to begin working on their university applications in just a few weeks, she explained. Then she asked each of them to share their preferred university with the class.

"Manchester," "Leeds," "Bristol," came the replies, to which she nodded approvingly.

When it was Asad's turn to speak, he hesitated, saying he was still undecided. He wasn't sure which of the dozens of universities he had researched online were official Brookhouse partners, and he didn't want to slip up and name one that wasn't on the list. Mrs. Chaudry moved on to the next student, but he could tell he had disappointed her.

Next she asked the assembled students if any had visited their preferred university, and a roomful of hands went up. Asad looked around bewildered. *These people have all been to the UK*, he thought. *What am I even doing here?*

His head was still spinning when he heard Mrs. Chaudry ask everyone to scan her a copy of their passports. She needed them on file. He wasn't sure if he should say anything. Surely she had read his application, which explained that he was a refugee. Surely she knew that refugees couldn't get passports, but that their identification papers could be used as travel documents. But what if this was going to cause a problem? What if he had been admitted by mistake? The thought had haunted him ever since he had received an email from Mr. Mulindi welcoming him to Brookhouse and another from Ajay saying he'd been awarded a Beacon Scholarship. After years of crushing disappointments, of false starts and missed opportunities, it seemed too good to be true. He decided not to call attention to himself, lest he trigger another setback. Maybe Mrs. Chaudry would forget about this and it would blow over.

. . .

From his first days on campus, it was clear to Asad that the well-to-do teenagers who were now his classmates had a different way of doing things. They ate whenever they were hungry, for instance, and many of them tossed their garbage onto the floor instead of in the rubbish bins that were provided in every room. The help would sweep it up when they came to do their rounds.

He was assigned to a "quad" room in Mandela House, the main boarding dormitory at the rear of campus, with three other IFY students: Denis, Julio, and Daniel Ngoria. Daniel was a scholarship kid like him, the only other student on financial aid in the entire IFY class of fifty, but Denis and Julio were more representative of their cohort. Denis's father was a member of parliament, and Julio's was the governor of Kakamega County, the region in western Kenya where Mr. Mulindi had grown up. The four roommates got along surprisingly well, given the close quarters and immense socioeconomic divide. But from the beginning there were little things that marked Denis and Julio as denizens of a different universe. They would order up mountains of Kentucky Fried Chicken for delivery, for instance, even though there was plenty of free food in the dining hall. And they were constantly leaving their expensive electronics unattended, as if they didn't worry that someone would steal them. Cameras, iPhones, video players—it was hard to keep track of all the costly gadgetry lying around.

There were other things that shocked Asad about his new environment as well. Not only did someone come to clean his room and take away his trash, there was an entire menu of meal options that he could choose from every day, and someone who would wash his dishes for him. Even his dirty laundry came back to the dorm room cleaned and pressed. And the small army of Brookhouse staff that kept the whole operation running was always exceedingly polite, greeting him with a smile and entreating him to "kindly" do this or that. They showed the students respect at all times. It was as if, Asad thought, "they were afraid you were the son of the president."

And Asad didn't let on that he wasn't. In fact, he refrained from telling anyone about his past in the first few weeks of school. In his experience, information asymmetry usually worked to his advantage; he would listen and learn from his new friends, but as he had done during the uncertain years in

Kisii, he offered up little about himself in return. He found that many of his classmates were eager to talk. They seemed desperate to unload about their problems, which in many cases boiled down to feeling neglected by busy parents or being denied money for this or that. In this bizarre, exclusive enclave, Asad felt like a sociologist studying the strange habits of the elite.

One girl in his IFY course complained about having to attend campaign events with her father, who was a prominent parliamentarian. Another boy, whose father was in real estate, lamented missing out on parties at a club called The Alchemist, where students with more permissive parents often congregated on the weekends. Asad had only a hazy sense of what clubs were, but he could tell they were of considerable importance. Cars were another frequent topic of conversation—makes and models, as well as the lessons and licensing required to drive them. He hadn't previously thought much about cars. They didn't feature centrally in his favorite literary works, although they were part of the background in some of the more recent novels he had read with middle-class protagonists. Kambili Achike, the narrator of Chimamanda Ngozi Adichie's *Purple Hibiscus*, is familiar enough with cars to recognize a Peugeot 504 by the roadside, for instance. But the cars themselves had never been the point. "These people are driving cars. End of story," he had thought to himself at the time. But to his classmates at Brookhouse, cars held a deeper meaning. They were important status symbols that enabled the haves to separate themselves from the have-nots, and perhaps more crucially, to determine which haves were separated from the have-nots by the greatest distance.

Cars even intruded on his coursework. In his economics class, the teacher explained the concept of Veblen goods, luxury items for which price and demand don't observe their usual inverse correlation, by comparing a Toyota and a Rolls-Royce. When a dealer knocks down the price of a Toyota, he can expect demand from ordinary consumers to increase. But part of the allure of a Rolls-Royce is that it's beyond the reach of regular people. Offer it at half-price, the teacher explained, and there may be less demand rather than more. Asad looked around the classroom to see if any of his fellow students looked as lost as he was, but all of them seemed to be following the lecture just fine. He quickly resolved to learn something about cars.

The IFY program followed an intensive, six-month curriculum developed by a consortium of mainly British universities, a kind of crash course for students from different educational backgrounds or who, as Asad discovered early on, had simply failed to meet the necessary standards for admission the first time around. The program loosely mirrored the British A-Level system, with students taking three main courses along with a writing or communications module designed to ensure proficiency in English. Asad had been expecting to feel out of his depth, having missed huge chunks of high school and spent the last two years mostly out of the classroom. And it was true that the Year Twelve and Thirteen students, who had been at Brookhouse the longest, were an impressive lot. They had clearly benefitted from a curriculum that asked more of students than the rote memorization that characterized the Kenyan national system—a system that in Asad's view delivered only the illusion of an education. But the IFY students were less polished. In addition to being pampered, they tended to have little interest in academics. Many of them felt compelled to attend university so as not to disappoint their parents.

This was a foreign notion to Asad, whose parents mostly valued education for its utility. Learning to read, write, and speak English, they knew, would make it easier to communicate with aid agencies and navigate the resettlement process. To the extent that they acknowledged Asad's less practical academic pursuits, they viewed them as oddities—strange quirks of their second son that they hoped wouldn't run him afoul of religious strictures. But the value of a Brookhouse education to those who were spending $20,000 a year to get one seemed to stem from something untethered to utility. After all, at least some of these students would never have to work a day in their lives. Education in their view, he decided, must be akin to a Veblen good.

Indeed, he could sense in the nonchalance of some of his schoolmates a subtle statement about class. They didn't need to work hard in school, because they could buy the pedigree that came with the Brookhouse name. That was off-putting, but in a strange way it offered a measure of reassurance. Far from the weakest student in their ranks, Asad quickly realized that he was in a position to excel. His writing and analytical skills put him far ahead of the pack in his two humanities courses. And while he had a lot of work to do in economics and business studies, neither of which he had had before, he knew he could outwork all of the other IFY kids. All of them except Daniel Ngoria, that was.

. . .

Life at Brookhouse adhered to a punishing schedule. Wakeup was at 6 a.m. for mandatory breakfast, followed by classes that ran from 8:15 a.m. to 3:35 p.m. on weekdays. After that students reported for various extracurricular activities—athletics, drama, or music, all of which carried extra fees—or signed in at a designated study area where they could be supervised by faculty or staff. Dinner was served from 6:30 p.m. to 7 p.m., after which there was exactly one hour and forty-five minutes of free time until students had to be back in their dorms. A brief study period preceded lights-out at 11 p.m.

As the fifth son of a nomadic herdsman in the remote and lawless region of West Pokot, near Kenya's border with Uganda, Daniel had grown up accustomed to a very different set of rhythms. His family had drifted with the seasons, wandering the scorched savannas in search of fertile grazing land and clashing frequently with murderous cattle raiders from the nearby Turkana region. Rival tribesmen had killed his grandfather and his father's second wife, and he and his brothers stood ready to retaliate. "It's the rule there," he explained. "Everyone has to protect the society and fight." Livestock is the closest thing to a bank account in Pokot culture, so protecting it is among the greatest responsibilities that can be bestowed on a man. Young *morans*, or warriors, spend months at a time in the bush watching over their flocks. It is dangerous, solitary work, and the only thing that kept Daniel from it was his slight build and timid disposition. His father regarded him as weak, useless when it came to protecting cattle from lions and hyenas. So when the government began to put pressure on tribal chiefs in the region to start sending at least one child per family to school, Daniel was the natural choice. Leaving his brothers to watch over the herd, he had gone away to primary school, a human token of good faith to the government and the first in his family to set foot in a classroom.

To everyone's surprise, Daniel had scored among the highest in the country on his final primary school exam. The distinction had earned him a scholarship from a charity called Wings to Fly, enabling him to attend one of the top national high schools in Nairobi. There he had won prestigious math and science competitions, and caught the eye of Brookhouse administrators, who offered him the lone fully funded place in the IFY program. On the day Mrs. Chaudry had asked each

student which UK university they hoped to attend, he had replied, "Manchester," without missing a beat.

By now Daniel was used to the rigidity of boarding school
life. Unlike his roommates Julio and Denis, he never slept
through breakfast or missed his first-period class. He was ad-
ept at multitasking, and had mastered the art of studying in the
brief passing periods between classes. As soon as dinner was
over, he would sling his black Hewlett-Packard-branded backpack over his shoulder and walk to the library, where he would
take his regular seat at the rectangular wooden table near the
door. Usually, Asad was already there.

Daniel had taken an immediate liking to his lean, bespectacled roommate with the angular Somali features. He noticed
that Asad rarely talked about himself, but that he had an easy
way of relating to even the most spoiled and big-headed kids on
campus. He seemed able to find just enough common ground
to forge a connection with anyone. Despite what most people assumed about the two scholarship kids, they shared little
aside from their outsider status—at least at first glance. Daniel was a Catholic, and a devout one at that, while Asad was
a Muslim who seemed to have more reverence for Nabokov
than for the written word of God. Their families shared some
broad cultural traits, having all descended from nomads, but
the contrasts largely outweighed the similarities. Under different circumstances, in fact, they might have fought each other
over grazing land. But at Brookhouse, it felt as if they spoke

a common language that only the two of them understood. Whenever their classmates would complain that the meat in the dining hall was too tough, or that the security guards were giving them a hard time about breaking curfew, they would look at each other and break into silent laughter. Who would have thought people could get so upset over such small things?

There were times when their shared unspoken language offered more than comic relief. Daniel never doubted that he belonged academically, but still he couldn't shake the feeling that socially he was intruding on a space that was reserved for others. "They anoint one or two of us to be among them every year," Asad had observed acidly soon after they met. The remark stuck with Daniel, lingering in the back of his mind every time he couldn't afford to answer a call from back home because he had run out of phone credit. Sometimes, his phone would ring again and again, and Denis or Julio would ask why he was ignoring his family. Asad never asked him that question. Instead, he would send Daniel a few dollars' worth of mobile money so he could replenish his account.

After only a few weeks of classes, Brookhouse closed down for half-term break and most of the boarding students went home. But home for Daniel was two or three days' drive in the rainy season, when the dirt roads in parts of rural Kenya melt into muddy rivers. Not wanting to spend the entire break in transit, and running short on cash in any case, he decided to stay on campus. Asad, he knew, had two younger siblings whom he looked after now that most of his family was in the United States. They lived in Eastleigh, which was an hour or two from Brookhouse by *matatu*. Asad had gone there as soon as school let out on Friday, but to Daniel's surprise, he reappeared the following day, carrying food for both of them to share. He did the same thing every day for the rest of the week, shuttling back and forth to school so his roommate wouldn't have to spend the holiday alone.

The two of them would go for long walks around campus, strolling between stone buildings overrun with bougainvillea and through lush gardens of bamboo and water lilies. Sometimes they would pause at the far end of the athletic fields, gazing back at the pitched roofs of the academic buildings, their Spanish tiles gouging perfect red triangles out of the gray-blue sky. It was on one of these walks that Daniel first learned that Asad had been to Somalia. Everything Daniel had ever read or seen on television about the country suggested a place where chaos and cruelty reigned. To hear the Kenyan media tell it, Somalis were all heartless extremists who reserved a special hatred for Kenya's open, cosmopolitan society. By now Daniel had met enough Somalis to know that wasn't true. But his image of Kenya's neighbor to the north remained that of a chaotic war zone, full of tanks and hulking armored personnel carriers the color of sand. It was crazy that Asad had actually been there. Truth be told, it was exhilarating to think he had seen it all up close and lived to tell the tale.

Daniel couldn't match his friend's stories—whether judged on content or delivery. Get Asad going on a topic and the words would just tumble out. It was as if all that listening he did around their classmates caused a backlog in his own communication system. But Daniel didn't mind that he sometimes couldn't get a word in edgewise. It was nice to be around someone who was as appreciative of their surroundings as he was, someone whose path to Brookhouse had been as unlikely as his—even if it had run through some very different places along the way.

...

Darkness had fallen over Brookhouse and the clamor of the day was finally receding into silence. Behind a long wooden desk piled high with papers, Mr. Mulindi was hard at work on a biology lesson. He was dressed in a dark suit and tie, his trademark plastic name tag hanging on a blue lanyard around his neck. On the walls and cabinets around him were the fruits of more than a decade of labor: abstract oil paintings, detailed etchings of a clock, a modernist sculpture of a dung beetle—all of it created by his beloved students.

A soft knock at the door pulled him away from his thoughts. There was little question of who it would be at this hour. Sure enough, in came two boys wearing backpacks and grins. Asad and Daniel had made a habit of visiting him in the evenings, when the day students had departed and the sounds of laughter and shouting no longer echoed through the halls. He could tell they viewed him as different from their other teachers, softer perhaps, and more reassuring. And he in turn saw them as different from the other students under his watch. "These were two boys shouldering a huge responsibility in addition to school," he recalled. "They were not like ordinary students here."

Mr. Mulindi was glad they had each other to lean on, and heartened to see they had become fast friends. They seemed to share the same values, despite different religious backgrounds, and to genuinely respect each other. But while Daniel was clearly sure about where he was headed, Asad seemed weighed down by doubt. He was struggling to catch up in some of his classes, economics in particular, and worried that his refugee status would ultimately prevent him from going to the UK. Mr. Mulindi knew that the latter worry had been fueled in part by Mrs. Chaudry, who had come to him in private to complain that Asad hadn't turned in a copy of his passport or alternative travel document and that as a result she hadn't been able to register him with the IFY's governing body. Accustomed to Mrs. Chaudry's pedantic ways, he hadn't given her grumbling much thought. Instead, he had brushed her off with a suggestion to reach out to the governing body directly and explain the situation. Surely, they would find a work-around, especially since Asad had the backing of the Beacon Scholarship.

But he could see now that the situation hadn't been resolved. Slouched on the sagging cushions of Mr. Mulindi's striped sofa, an exasperated Asad recounted his latest run-in with Mrs. Chaudry: Several weeks had passed since her initial request for the passports, and she had given the class a final deadline after which they wouldn't be allowed to enroll at all. When Asad had finally gotten up the courage to explain his situation, she had responded angrily that it was far too late to bring up something as important as this. "You're just telling me this now?" he recalled her saying. "You can't register for this program without a passport. I'm sorry, you need to be able to travel to the UK."

Mr. Mulindi listened patiently as Asad unburdened himself. Then he placed a reassuring hand on his shoulder and told him to focus on his schoolwork. The situation with Mrs. Chaudry would be resolved, he said, and if it came to it, he would to go to the Ministry of Interior himself to lobby for a travel document. "Do your best in your studies," he said, "because I'm one hundred percent sure doors will open."

X

MIRACLE

Nairobi, Kenya, December 2017

There was a long line of students waiting to check in when Asad arrived at school with his graphing calculator and two No. 2 pencils. It was 7:45 on a cloudy Saturday morning, but Brookhouse was already pulsing with nervous energy. High school juniors and seniors from across the country had come to take the SAT, the grueling four-hour aptitude test required for admission to most universities in the United States. By definition, the students were all exceptional, having set their sights on an academic goal that only a tiny fraction of Kenyans would ever attempt. Most had probably been studying for months, if not years, diligently working through fat books of practice exams and spending hours each week with private tutors.

Asad had learned of the SAT just three and a half weeks

earlier. Both Brookhouse and the Beacon funneled students to mainly British universities, but he had never quite let go of the idea of going to America. When he typed "best university writing programs" into Google, the same U.S. colleges popped up on list after list: Harvard, Columbia, Princeton, the University of Iowa. When he clicked through to their websites, he saw photos of black students as well as white students, usually smiling and laughing together. If not quite familiar, they looked at least welcoming. And the generous, need-blind admissions policies most of them advertised seemed tailored to people like him. By contrast, the British universities he looked up offered fewer need-based scholarships, and their student bodies appeared whiter and wealthier.

These were potentially crucial differences. Ajay had been clear that his Beacon Scholarship wasn't guaranteed after the first year at Brookhouse: He would have to earn its renewal with high grades in the IFY program. Even admission to a partner university wouldn't guarantee continued support from the Beacon. The scholarship received dozens of worthy applicants every year, and it couldn't say yes to all of them. So Asad decided to apply to U.S. universities at the same time as he sought to renew his Beacon Scholarship and win admission to a British university, even though doing so would mean double the work. Among the first things he discovered when he began researching how to apply to American colleges, however, was the daunting SAT requirement.

Aside from the national high school exam and the IQ test Dr. Sue had given him, he had never taken a standardized test. Back in Dadaab, there had been no regular assessments. Even ordinary subject tests in math and science had been rare, since both teachers and testing materials like blue books had been in short supply.

Determined to do his best, he went in search of a book of practice SATs. He tried the sidewalk booksellers in Eastleigh, where years ago he had bought his copy of *Half a Day and Other Stories*. When he couldn't find one there, he tried a second-hand bookstore in the central business district. The rows of sagging shelves were stocked with dusty self-help books and study guides, most of them years out of print, but none of them covered the SAT. Finally, he tried Yaya Center, the same mall where he had ridden his first escalator. On the second floor was an expensive bookstore where crisp new volumes came sheathed in plastic shrink-wrap, so you couldn't leaf through them. There he found a copy of *The Official SAT Study Guide* published by the College Board. It was enormous, much larger than any book he had ever owned. It was also $35, more money than he had brought with him, so he had to come back to buy it the following day.

What he found inside the book was even more dispiriting. The eight full-length exams from previous years were sprinkled with material he vaguely recognized: linear equations, geome-try, and even some passages from books by Virginia Woolf and

F. Scott Fitzgerald. But the questions might as well have been in a foreign language. They were phrased in convoluted ways and required you to infer things about the authors' intentions that seemed impossible to know. Some of the reading comprehension passages were about such obscure topics that he found them difficult to follow. What did he know about the relative migratory patterns of loggerhead turtles versus reed warblers— and what was a reed warbler anyhow? Often, he would get so absorbed in the passages that he would forget to look at the questions, getting to the end only to realize he was no closer to having the answers. "Complete bewilderment," was how he described his initial reaction to the test. "The whole thing just seemed bizarre to me."

The rapid pace at which he was supposed to read and digest the information was also a problem. He had spent much of his life buried in books, but never with a stopwatch running in the back of his mind. Having to race through the passages took the fun out of reading. It also made him anxious and sloppy. He would miss the names of the protagonists or other key pieces of information. Inevitably, he would run out of time before the end of the section. Sometimes there were entire rows of blank circles still staring back at him from the answer sheet when the alarm on his phone buzzed, indicating that time was up.

Asad knew he wasn't fully prepared on the morning of the exam, but he had read all 792 pages of the study guide—most of them more than once. Maybe more of it had seeped into his brain than he was giving himself credit for. Maybe he would surprise himself and do all right.

He was shocked by the number of students who had turned up to take the test, and by the seriousness of the test administrators. Most of the administrators were white, and he could tell from their accents that they were Americans. They checked each student's ID and test registration, and inspected their watches, pencils, and calculators. Then they patted the test-takers down as if they were guarding a high-security facility. "Wow, I guess they assume we are all criminals," Asad thought to himself. But in addition to mild resentment, he felt something akin to relief. Cheating was rampant on the national exams in Kenya. At least this would be a fair fight.

So many students had registered for the SAT that they had to be divided between multiple classrooms. Asad found a seat in a classroom near the back of the campus, across the grassy quad from Mandela House, and squeezed into a desk with a wooden top that opened like a lid. He tried to listen carefully as the test invigilator read through a long list of instructions. But soon his mind began to wander and the litany of directives about answer sheets and bathroom breaks was drifting past him like idle chatter over a cooking fire. At last, he heard the invigilator say, "You may now open your test booklets to Section One, read the instructions, and begin." Suddenly the room was filled with the sound of dozens of flimsy pages turning at once.

· · ·

Applying to Brookhouse and the Beacon had been confusing and at times infuriating. But compared to the U.S. college application process, it had been relatively straightforward. After weeks of online research, Asad had compiled a list of nine U.S. colleges. At the top of the list were Harvard, Princeton, and Stanford, all of which he had heard of before arriving at Brookhouse. In addition, he had settled on the University of Pennsylvania, Dartmouth, Williams, Wesleyan, Bowdoin, and Whitman—a tiny liberal arts college in eastern Washington, not far from where Maryan lived. All nine were highly selective. Some, like Harvard and Princeton, admitted as few as 6 percent and 7 percent of applicants, respectively. But there was little point in applying to less competitive colleges, he had been advised. Only those at the top of the heap had the financial resources to give scholarships to foreign applicants.

All of the schools he had chosen accepted the Common Application, a website that hosts application materials for hundreds of U.S. colleges and, in theory at least, simplifies the process. As with the Brookhouse application, the Common App asked for lots of things he didn't have: official transcripts, employment details for his parents, a credit card with which to pay the $75 to $100 fee for each application he submitted. For the most part, these were shortcomings he could work around, fudging the details here and there and leaning on the Abdis and other, more affluent friends who had come into his life in the wake of the *New York Times* article for financial support. Had he been back in the camp where no one had a bank account, there would have been no way to apply; he would have simply been shut out.

Even with a borrowed credit card there was still one deficiency he wasn't sure he could overcome: citizenship. A little red asterisk next to the question indicated that it was required, but the drop-down menu gave no option for refugees or stateless people. He scrolled down a list of what seemed like every country in the world. Nothing described him, not even a field marked "other" or "none." With no option to provide a written addendum, he felt at a loss. "I have a long story. I need to explain this," he thought.

The Common App seemed to be forcing him into a lie, but what if it was held against him later in the process? What if Harvard or Stanford reacted the way Mrs. Chaudry had, angrily rebuking him for having hid the fact that he was a refugee? He decided that claiming Somali citizenship amounted to a smaller lie than claiming Kenyan citizenship, since the former hadn't explicitly disowned him. He selected "Somalia," and resolved to make his refugee status extra clear in the essay portion of the application.

In some ways, American colleges seemed attuned to the needs of disadvantaged students like him—offering fee waivers and scholarships, for instance. But in other ways, they appeared oblivious to the financial barriers their own procedures created. In order to apply for financial aid, many colleges required him to create a CSS profile, a detailed financial report that cost $25 to submit to the first college and $16 to submit to every college thereafter. Here he was literally begging for money, and yet he was expected to have at least some financial resources already.

As he read through the CSS questionnaire, it became clear that being poor in America meant something very different than being poor in Kenya. Among the details he was expected to provide were the type and value of any investments, trusts, or retirement assets he had. Did he or a parent own a business or a farm? Did they own any real estate beyond their primary home, such as a seasonal or vacation house? Near the bottom of the form was a section marked "Special Circumstances," which allowed applicants to explain any sudden change in their family fortunes—the result of illness or job loss, for instance. Compared to the sections on income and assets, which he had mostly populated with zeros, this one seemed more relevant to him. While the boxes marked "exceptional medical or dental expenses" and "siblings in private school" didn't apply, the one marked "catastrophic event or natural disaster" seemed to fit. He ticked it and typed a brief explanation in the field below:

I was born in Dadaab refugee camp in Kenya to parents who are themselves refugees. We do not own any land or have any income. My parents were resettled in the United States in 2017 and they now live on public assistance. Because of my refugee status, I am not allowed to work. I do not even belong to any country. I do not pay any tax. Neither do my parents. I hereby request to be considered for financial aid.

There were other aspects of the admissions process that underscored the distance between his world and the world inhabited by the typical applicant. In addition to the Common App, most of the colleges on his list required their own "supplemental" applications that called for additional essays. "In what way do you see a liberal arts education having practical value?" Wesleyan asked of its applicants. What is your "favorite keepsake or memento?" Princeton wanted to know. But strangest of all were the questions about the colleges themselves: "How will you explore your intellectual and academic interests at the University of Pennsylvania?" or "Why Harvard?"

Why Harvard? he thought. *I will go to any of these colleges! All of their students are better off than refugees in Kenya!*

But there were other essay questions that made more sense and that he enjoyed answering. Asked to reflect on an event that changed the course of his life, he wrote about that day in second grade when his English teacher, Halima, sent him home with instructions to buy a second notebook. The memory of his father, teary eyed, telling him he could learn to write in the dust still "juts out like a knot in my net of memories from Dadaab refugee camp," he wrote. "In a way, I followed my father's advice, taking my education wherever I could get it." Another prompt asked about a person who had influenced him in a significant way. "I owe everything I am today to my sister, Maryan, who surrendered her dreams to tend to mine, as one would for a seedling," he wrote.

...

A week or so before the Common App was due, Mr. Mulindi was at his parents' home in rural western Kenya. It was Christmastime and his entire extended family had gathered, as they do each holiday season, to celebrate the end of the year and the beginning of the next, which they hoped would bring even greater blessings. Cousins, uncles, and aunties, one of whom had just turned 102, came from across the country with their children and grandchildren—three generations reunited in their ancestral homeland. The mood was festive, lifted by the familiar sights and sounds of a village that had changed remarkably little since Mr. Mulindi was a teenager sleeping in his shoes: children running barefoot over freshly tilled soil, troops of cheeky monkeys chiding them from the trees.

One evening as the family prepared a hearty meal of chicken and goat meat, Mr. Mulindi's phone chimed with an urgent text message from Asad: Could he please write a letter of recommendation before the deadline on January 1? Had it been anyone else making a last-minute request that would pull him away from his family, Mr. Mulindi might have demurred. Like most Kenyans who spend the holidays up-country, he was accustomed to being undisturbed. There was a time when he would have been unreachable during these few precious weeks of the year. As it was, he was still out of range of the Internet. He would have to travel nearly an hour by bus to the nearest town, where a lone cyber café offered the only portal to the web for miles. But ever since their first meeting, he had been quietly rooting for Asad, and in the short time they had gotten to know each other, he had grown unusually attached to the boy. He felt proud, protective even, of this young man whom so many of his colleagues had doubted at first.

After he had learned of the passport issue with Mrs. Chaudry, Mr. Mulindi had been surprised by how irritated he felt: *Here we are trying to be as supportive as we can of this boy, but the course leader is telling him he doesn't belong,* he thought. The next day he pulled Mrs. Chaudry aside and asked her to write to the IFY governing body right away to resolve the issue. It was an outwardly courteous exchange, but inside he was still feeling cross. The relief he felt a few days later upon hearing that Asad had finally been enrolled, manually and without a passport, had been equally outsize, almost as if Asad was his own son.

When he thought about it, part of their connection was readily explicable. As a boy, Mr. Mulindi had struggled in school, especially in mathematics, and as a teacher, he found himself drawn to the students who faced the longest odds. "When I see a child who is struggling, in a way I see myself through them," he said. Asad was straining to make up for lost time, and to overcome his lack of formal schooling, especially in economics. But in other ways, he was very different from the students Mr. Mulindi usually took under his wing. He was disciplined and thoughtful, a principled adult in a school full of spoiled children. He had been on campus just a few short weeks, but already he was emerging as a quiet leader. "He wasn't a lone ranger," Mr. Mulindi recalled. "The younger children saw him as a big brother." The more of this side of Asad that Mr. Mulindi observed, the more convinced he became of Asad's unusual promise—and the more compelled he felt to smooth the path ahead for him.

Still, Mr. Mulindi had his doubts. The average SAT scores required to get into the colleges Asad had selected were near perfect. Could Asad really be expected to compete after just a few weeks of practice? Then again, who would have thought a poor boy from Kakamega could have become the headmaster of the Brookhouse School? "I don't want to kill his spirit," Mr. Mulindi thought as he made his way to the cyber café. "I wouldn't want to be a person who stood in his way when there was an opportunity coming up."

. . .

Doubt was welling up inside of Asad, too. The SAT hadn't gone well. That much he knew as soon as he left the exam. Out of the four main sections, he hadn't finished a single one. Even worse, he had left dozens of questions blank on his answer sheet—forgetting that if he simply guessed he would have a one-in-four chance of getting them right. But two weeks later, when he signed in to the College Board's website, the results that greeted him were even worse than he had imagined. "I'm quite illiterate, but I read a lot," Salinger's Caulfield says in *The Catcher in the Rye*. He doesn't mean it, of course, and maybe, deep down, Asad didn't, either. But for days he couldn't get that line out of his head. How was it possible that he had spent *this* much of his life reading and still have done *this* badly? Maybe his C+ on the national exam hadn't been an aberration. Maybe he just wasn't very smart.

There were other reasons to think he was out of his depth. In addition to Mr. Mulindi's reference, he needed one from the school counselor. But when he emailed Otieno Milafu, who as Brookhouse's college advisor assisted all of the IFY students with their university applications, he had gotten a decidedly chilly reply. "This will be a very rushed application and will not help much," Mr. Milafu had written, adding that U.S. universities that offered scholarships required high SAT scores as well as "a good level of community service involvement." He would fill out the reference form if Asad insisted, he said, but he "strongly advised" focusing on the IFY program and then taking a "gap year" before applying to U.S. colleges.

A gap year? Community service? The more Asad learned about the college application process the more absurd it seemed. He knew some of his classmates volunteered in places like Kibera, a vast and impoverished Nairobi slum where, except for the skyscrapers in the distance, life was not so different from Dadaab. What he hadn't realized was that doing so would help them get into college. What a world, he thought, in which generosity was such a rare quality among the rich that a little slum tourism was enough to make you stand out.

By the time he was finally ready to submit his applications, he had convinced himself that there was little point. "It's just one more thing you're trying," he told himself. He had tried for so many things over the years that hadn't worked out. This would be no different.

But a few weeks after he arrived back at school in mid-January, something happened that reignited a flicker of hope. His mid-semester report card came back better than expected: all A's and B's—and even a B in economics! Not long after that, he found out he had been made a boarding prefect, one of the highest nonacademic honors at Brookhouse. It meant he was responsible for the other boys in his dorm, charged with enforcing the rules and mediating disputes. More than that, though, it meant he belonged. He was a Brookhouse boy now—not some charity case, but a respected member of the community who had been entrusted with upholding its values. If a school like this had accepted him, wasn't there a chance a university in the United States would too?

He had gone to see Mr. Milafu in person soon after arriving back on campus, and it turned out that the college advisor wasn't so callous or exacting after all. An avuncular middle-aged man whose subtly buoyant demeanor made Asad question whether he was really the same person he had corresponded with over email, Mr. Milafu was open and generous with his time. The two of them fell into a long conversation about Brookhouse, and the unusual path Asad had taken to get there. Mr. Milafu seemed impressed when he heard that Asad had been made a prefect, and he promised to mention it, along with the better-than-expected grades, in his mid-year report to the universities to which Asad had applied.

With things beginning to look up in the first weeks of the year, Asad decided to revisit the SAT. The test was offered again in March. With more time to practice, perhaps he could boost his score. The results would be reported too late for some but not all of the colleges to take into account, and if he wound up on a waiting list, a higher score might be enough to push him over the top. But almost immediately his plan began to veer off course. By the time he tried to sign up, the Brook-house location was already full. The nearest alternative test center was at a Christian boarding school in a small town on the eastern escarpment of the Great Rift Valley, at least half a day's drive from Nairobi by *matatu*. He would have to borrow money for the trip, take a day off from school, and spend the night before the exam in the Rift Valley—yet another expense he wasn't sure how he would cover. Reluctantly, he signed up anyway and began working his way through *The Official SAT Study Guide* for a second time.

A little more than two weeks before he was supposed to

take the exam, he hit another snag: On February 21, he got an email from the College Board asking him to answer a few questions as part of a "verification" exercise to ensure that he was taking the test for one of its "intended purposes"—applying to a college, scholarship, or financial aid program that required the SAT. Even before the deadline for submitting the questionnaire had passed, he received a second email informing him that his registration for the March exam had been cancelled and that he had been re-registered for the May exam—long after the colleges he had applied to would have made their admission decisions. By way of explanation, the College Board cited a new security policy designed to "provide a fair testing environment for all test takers." Asad had no idea why his presence might jeopardize the fairness of the exam for other takers, but he couldn't help but wonder if the combination of his age and his ethnicity had prompted the extra scrutiny.

Confused and angry, he contacted the College Board to see if he could get reinstated. After a long back-and-forth, he was finally re-registered for the March exam. But when he arrived at the test center in the Rift Valley on the appointed day, having traveled much of the previous day to get there, he was turned away at the door. He had his registration form in hand, but the test invigilators couldn't find his name on the roster of registered students. Several frantic telephone calls later, he discovered that he had been re-registered at the Brookhouse location, not the one in the Rift Valley. Asad was crestfallen.

He had spent weeks preparing to retake the test and neglecting his Brookhouse studies—all of it seemingly for nothing.

But he wasn't ready to give up yet. Over the next few days, he spent hours on the phone and on email pleading to be allowed a makeup exam. Eventually, some of his friends took to Twitter to lobby the College Board on his behalf. Several high-profile journalists who had read his articles lent their support to the social media campaign, including reporters at the *New York Times* and the *New Yorker*. Almost immediately, the College Board's representatives began to sound more accommodating: "I [am] working to explore options for a make-up exam for you and would like to know what your preferred testing center(s) would be," a customer care specialist named Iain Wickerson wrote soon after the tweets, some of which were critical of the College Board, began to ricochet across the Internet.

In the end, Asad got his makeup exam. Two weeks later, he took the nearly four-hour test again, this time by himself in an empty Brookhouse classroom. His score improved on both sections, but not by as much as he had hoped. It was hardly a resounding success, but it wasn't a failure either. He had given it everything he had. Now there was nothing left to do except wait.

. . .

The first rejection came at 4 a.m. on Friday, March 2 (3 p.m. the day before in Walla Walla, Washington). Asad had waited up, unable to sleep knowing the Whitman College admissions decisions would be posted online overnight. Whitman wasn't his top choice—far from it. But it was the least selective school on his list: nearly half of all applicants had been accepted the previous year, and unusual among top liberal arts colleges, it didn't require the SAT. If he had a prayer of getting in anywhere, it was there. But it was a brief, apologetic message that awaited him in the web portal that night: "We appreciate the time you spent learning about Whitman and gave your application careful consideration. While we are honored to have received more applications than we have space to admit in a small entering class, the unfortunate result is that we are unable to offer admission to you and many other talented students."

More rejections came in the following days and weeks. First Williams, then Penn, Dartmouth, Wesleyan, and Bowdoin. Each one left him feeling more deflated. "The future doesn't look very bright for me," he wrote glumly to a friend one day.

By the end of March, there were only three schools left that he hadn't heard from: Harvard, Stanford, and Princeton. On the day the Harvard and Princeton decisions were due, he went to visit an old friend from his earliest days in Nairobi, mostly as a way to distract himself from the agony of waiting. Dakane was a college student at the University of Nairobi, and he lived with his sister in a modest apartment. The two friends stayed up late into the night talking about Kenyan politics. A disputed election in one of the country's northern counties was making headlines, and Dakane felt strongly that the losing candidate had been cheated. Asad didn't have an opinion either way, and he was only half-listening to his friend anyway. Later that night, after Dakane had gone to bed, Asad lay awake in the darkened apartment counting down the hours. He couldn't sleep and he couldn't read. He couldn't do anything except obsess about the verdict looming over him. It would either change his life forever—or condemn him to at least another year of waiting.

At exactly 3 a.m. he punched his email and password into the Harvard applicant portal. Then he tapped the "log-in" button and held his breath as he waited for the page to load. More bad news: his seventh straight rejection. "So this is it," he thought, the high of his adrenaline rush cratering into a feeling of bitter resignation. "There is no hope now."

For a moment, he thought about going to sleep. There was no need to check the Princeton decision; he already knew what it said. But something propelled him to retrieve the letter just in case. And as he gazed at the orange Tiger mascot on the screen of his Samsung, it took a moment to process what he was reading: "Congratulations! I am delighted to offer you admission to Princeton's Class of 2022," the letter began. Suddenly, fireworks were exploding inside his chest. He leapt off of the couch and shook Dakane awake. He wanted to be sure he wasn't dreaming, that his friend could see what he could see: a full scholarship, worth $70,000 a year.

A moment later he was on the phone with Maryan. She didn't know what Princeton was, but she understood what the scholarship meant: her brother was coming to America. She sobbed and he sobbed. Both of them knew that something miraculous had occurred. In the coming days and weeks, he would learn that Toni Morrison and John McPhee taught at Princeton. She had won the Nobel Prize for literature and he the Pulitzer Prize. Both were writers that Asad had idolized for years. There was no way to explain what any of that meant to his family, though, so he started telling them something else: "I'm going to Michelle Obama's school."

...

For days after he received the acceptance letter, Asad was in a daze. He reread it over and over, unable to fully accept that it was real. And for hours at a time, he gazed at online photographs of Princeton's magnificent New Jersey campus. A dreamscape of resplendent stone archways and towering Gothic spires, it looked like something out of *Harry Potter*. It was hard to imagine buildings like that existed anywhere, much less that he would soon live and study among them.

Things got even more surreal when he started getting calls from reporters. He had tweeted word of his acceptance just minutes after receiving the news: "Many people, in Dadaab and beyond, made this possible and I am indebted to all, but it was my sister Maryan who first let me dream," he had written. Now, he was getting inquiries from Voice of America, the BBC Somali Service, and the *Daily Nation* and other Kenyan news outlets, all of which wanted to hear from the boy from Dadaab who had made it into the world's top-ranked university. "From Refugee Camp, Young Somali Lands Spot at Princeton," read one headline. "Dreams are valid!! ASAD HUSSEIN, refugee from Dadaab, accepted by prestigious Princeton University," read another.

But even before the initial shock had faded, a flurry of emails from Princeton administrators brought him back down to earth. They were from the staff of the Davis International Center and they laid out the gargantuan list of tasks that stood between him and a U.S. visa. Forms with names like I-20 and D-160 needed to be completed and returned urgently. Even more pressingly, he needed to contact UNHCR about getting a conventional travel document, a kind of passport for the stateless that would allow him to travel to the United States. As his to-do list exploded with tasks that were complicated by his refugee status, it became clear that he still had a long way to go.

The biggest immediate problem was the conventional travel document. Like most refugees living in Kenya, Asad only had one official form of identification, his family's food ration card, which listed his name alongside those of his parents and siblings. Before UNHCR would issue him a conventional travel document, however, the organization required him to prove he had been born in Kenya. Doing that would be extremely difficult, because like thousands of refugees born in Dadaab, he had never been issued a birth certificate. He didn't exist in the official Kenyan register, and there was seemingly no way to prove he belonged there. Like a thought criminal in *Nineteen Eighty-Four*, it was as if he had been "unpersoned."

The closest thing to a birth certificate he had was an old medical form. Worn and yellowed with age, it showed he had received several immunizations at the hospital in Ifo sometime before his first birthday. It was compelling evidence, he was told, but likely not enough for Kenya's Department of Refugee Affairs, which jointly issued the travel documents with UNHCR. He would need to swear an affidavit saying he had been born in Kenya, and get another from a Kenyan citizen who could vouch for him. Both would need the seal of an official Kenyan notary.

While Asad was researching affidavits and notaries, he received yet another piece of distressing news: Ajay had found out about his Princeton acceptance from an article in the news and apparently felt angry and betrayed. Ajay had said that Asad should have a Plan B in case his Beacon Scholarship wasn't renewed. But his Plan B had just become his Plan A, assuming he could get a U.S. visa, and in his initial state of euphoria he hadn't thought to tell Ajay in person. Now he was reading a long, bullet-pointed email from the Beacon founder that seemed both intended to dissuade him from accepting Princeton's offer and remind him that he couldn't count on the Beacon Scholarship.

"We are aware of quite a few of what are often called 'free

ride' (100 percent) scholarships in a number of U.S. universities. Indeed there are some agents in Africa who specialize in obtaining these for African students. Our research, and that done by others, comes up with mixed views about these scholarships . . . but there are clear motivations behind them, including diversity, etc.," the email read in part. "We also believe that our Scholars must gain entry to schools and universities on a level playing field, i.e., they must be as good or better than the cohort that has gained admission at the same time. We do not ask for schools or universities to make allowances on their admission grade tariffs. This means that our Scholars begin with the confidence of knowing they are good enough to be at a particular school or university. This is quite a different approach, and ensures that only top students are supported, and put on the pathway." Ajay went on to say that Asad was currently on a shortlist for the next year's Beacon Scholarship, along with "a number of excellent candidates who are competing for one Beacon Scholarship at each of five UK universities." He would be "assessed alongside the other candidates," but there was "no guarantee" that he would be successful.

Asad was stunned. Clearly Ajay didn't believe he had earned his spot at Princeton on merit. Nor did he sound reassuring about Asad's prospects of continuing on the Beacon. On the contrary, it seemed as if by offending Ajay, Asad may have severed a lifeline—one he would desperately need if the United States denied his visa application.

The tenor of his interactions with Ajay and other Beacon Scholarship administrators changed markedly after that. Where he had once felt warmth and enthusiasm, he now felt cold professionalism. He apologized to Dr. Sue over the phone, but even she seemed to take Ajay's side. She said that of course she wanted what was best for him, but she didn't understand why he hadn't told her about his applications to U.S. colleges or why she had had to learn of his Princeton acceptance from Voice of America. Still, Dr. Sue was happy for Asad, and she broke down in tears and embraced him the next time they saw each other in person.

Roughly two weeks later, Asad attended a leadership workshop with the other Beacon Scholars. Afterward, he received a note of personalized feedback from the administrators. They admonished him for being "checked out" and said his "presence wasn't felt." Asad didn't think that was true; he had done his best to engage with the other scholars, and they had even selected him to lead a group presentation. Frustrated, he searched through his email inbox for the feedback he had received after a previous workshop, just two months earlier. "Friendly and well liked despite being an older scholar. He makes everyone feel special," it read in part. He had also been commended for being "thorough and well organized" and for his "good and creative negotiation skills." The one area the administrators had flagged for improvement was in finding "creative and polite ways to give difficult/hard feedback."

It seemed as if Ajay was laying the groundwork to cut him loose from the program. Asad tried not to let the situation bother him, but it didn't sit right. He felt angry and worried and guilty all at once: "Man, they are torturing me!" he thought. It didn't help that he kept running into problems trying to get his travel document. He spent a week gathering the affidavits, and a whole day at the Department of Refugee Affairs filling out forms and getting fingerprinted, only to find out that one of the affidavits he had prepared didn't meet the department's standards. Not just any Kenyan could vouch for his birth in the country; it needed to be a medical professional. Luckily, one of the Abdis, Abdinasir Amin, had a PhD in public health and could sign the document. Still, Asad had to start the whole process over again. And the longer it took, the more the people at the Davis International Center fretted. The more they fretted, the more he worried that he wouldn't make it to Princeton after all. If that happened, he thought, it would be nice to be able to fall back on the Beacon Scholarship.

But sure enough, a few weeks later, the news he had been dreading arrived in his inbox: "Having given careful consideration to your Assessment Report, and observed your interactions with other candidates and Beacon Scholars at the Teambuilding Workshop, we feel that your overall profile and qualities are not as strong as those of other candidates, and I regret that we are therefore unable to consider your application further." And just like that the safety net had been ripped out from under him. Now everything hinged on his U.S. visa application.

. . .

The U.S. Embassy in Nairobi sits a safe 100 feet back from United Nations Avenue, shielded from the already protected diplomatic enclave of Gigiri by heavy concrete walls. The towering fortresslike structure sprawls over 125,000 square feet, every inch of it built to withstand an explosion as powerful as the one that destroyed the Twin Towers on 9/11. Although it opened during George W. Bush's presidency, a more fitting symbol of America's fearful inward turn under Trump would have been difficult to imagine.

On the day Asad arrived for his visa appointment, the line to pass through the initial security check stretched nearly a quarter mile around the block. Hundreds of people, many of them dressed in their Sunday best—suits, ties, and freshly shined shoes—waited patiently in the clear mid-morning sun. It looked as if it would take an hour at least to reach the front, where security guards were inspecting people's IDs and waving them down with magnetic wands. But Asad had been in line for only a few moments when a man in a dark suit and tie emerged from inside the embassy and called his name. Young and affable, the man waved him past the security check and through a set of steel-reinforced doors toward a metal detector.

After two more trips to the Department of Refugee Affairs, Asad had finally managed to get his travel document.

But getting an F-1 student visa would require yet another stroke of luck. Like all other applicants for nonimmigrant visas, he needed to convince the consular officer at the embassy that he wouldn't overstay his visa or try to remain illegally in the United States. As a refugee with no assets or property in Kenya, and with family in the United States, that was going to be difficult. But an even bigger impediment was the Trump travel ban. Its scope had been narrowed as a result of the legal challenges, but the ban still applied to Somali nationals. In theory, it shouldn't apply to him as a stateless person who had been born in Kenya. But there was enough ambiguity that Princeton had hired a law firm to make his case. The memo the lawyers had submitted on his behalf was fifteen pages long, including supporting documents. If they were that worried, he knew he should be worried too.

Once through the metal detector, he followed a concrete footpath to a second waiting area, and from there into a dimly lit room with a row of teller-like windows running the length of the back wall. Behind the tall glass panes, consular officers shuffled papers and tapped intermittently on their keyboards. This was it for Asad, the final judgment that would either make his Princeton acceptance real or reveal it as a painful illusion. He had steeled himself for a tough grilling, and rehearsed answers to every conceivable line of questioning. He was ready to explain his trip to Somalia, to dispel concerns about possible extremist ties, and to state his responsibilities to his younger siblings—and his intention to return to Nairobi after gradua-tion to care for them. But the man in the suit and tie didn't ask him about any of these things. Instead, he waved Asad over to the farthest teller window with a smile. "What are you plan-ning to study?" he asked, eyeballing the heap of documents Asad had handed him from Princeton. It turned out that the man had grown up in New Jersey and gone to the University of Pennsylvania before joining the Foreign Service. He seemed impressed that Asad had been admitted to Princeton, and apol-ogetic about the Trump administration's immigration policies. After a few more moments of small talk, he said Asad was all set and that his visa would be ready in a few days.

When it was over, Asad couldn't believe it had been that easy. "It's like I've been fully upgraded to a human being," he thought as he sailed out of the embassy, his feet barely touch-ing the ground. After twenty-two years in limbo, he had finally broken free. But as the initial shock faded and he began to pro-cess what it all meant, the joy of having finally outrun his past gave way to feelings of sadness and guilt. He was headed to America, but his younger siblings were not. During his time at Brookhouse, he had been able to keep one eye on Abdi Malik and Habiba. He had kept food on the table and hounded them to stay in school. Aged eighteen and fourteen, they would now be on their own.

Book Three

REFLECTIONS

XI

AMERICA AT LAST

New York, July 2018

By the time Asad arrived at John F. Kennedy International Airport in New York, I had known him for a little more than a year and a half. What had started with an article in *Foreign Policy*, where he had written about Trump's travel ban, had become an extended collaboration on a book about his life, and, over time, a close friendship. To say it had been a roller-coaster ride would be a radical understatement. In the taxi ride into the city, threading our way through light traffic on the Brooklyn-Queens Expressway, I still couldn't quite believe Asad had made it here, or that he was sitting next to me.

It felt like only yesterday that I was in the café on the ground floor of Yaya Center, hearing his story for the first time. Back then, he had been about to start his first semester at United States International University Africa, while he waited for his parents' green cards to come through. He had seemed so wounded by the travel ban, yet so irrepressibly optimistic about everything else. Insatiable—that's how he had struck me. Driven to learn as much as he could about as many things as he could, no matter that no one had ever been interested in him. Like all first impressions, it was fragmentary and superficial. But all these months later, it still rang true.

Soon after that initial meeting, Asad and I had begun meeting frequently for long, informal interviews at a café in the Westlands neighborhood of Nairobi that he referred to as my "office." But then one day in early autumn, after we had been meeting for more than six months, he suddenly stopped responding. I called, texted, and messaged him on Twitter, but it was as if he had vanished. I thought perhaps he had had second thoughts about letting me write about him. I was disappointed, but didn't think much of it at the time. I was busy reporting on the migration crisis that was roiling Europe and turning Libya into a haven for modern slavery. I hadn't met Bekar yet, but I was writing about the kinds of perilous journeys his older brothers had taken—only from West Africa and the Sahel region, through the Sahara Desert to Libya's Mediterranean coast.

It wasn't long, however, before I found myself thinking about Asad again. A few weeks after I returned from the Sahara, I happened to meet a woman named Susan Kiragu at a panel event on the foreign aid industry in Nairobi. She said she had done a PhD at Cambridge and joined the faculty there, but grown disillusioned with academia because so many of her colleagues seemed to lack "moral imagination." She wanted to help people, not just study them. So she had quit her job at Cambridge and founded an educational charity, and later, a school in her parents' hometown in the Rift Valley. She also mentioned a scholarship she helped to administer. It was for poor but gifted Kenyans, several of whom had followed in her footsteps to Cambridge. The Beacon Scholarship, she said it was called.

Listening to Dr. Sue, I was reminded of something Asad had told me back at our very first meeting. When he let slip that he had never been to university, I had wondered aloud whether there might be a scholarship fund in Britain or the United States that would support a student like him. After all, how many twenty-one-year-olds—let alone twenty-one-year-old refugees—had written essays in the *New York Times*? He said that, actually, the president of one Oxford college *had* read his *Times* piece and written to him suggesting that he apply. But when Asad had written back to ask whether he would be eligible even without proper immigration papers, he had never heard back. I mentioned this to Dr. Sue, and relayed what I knew of Asad's story in brief, adding that he had disappeared suddenly and that I wasn't sure I would be able to track him down. Assuming we could contact him, though, I asked if the Beacon might consider supporting him. Dr. Sue's face lit up immediately. Later, we exchanged contact information and I typed Asad's email address and number into her phone.

A few weeks later, I finally heard from Asad. He had been in Somalia with Bekar, but hadn't told me because he knew I would have tried to dissuade him from going. Dr. Sue called me several days after that, saying that she had managed to connect with Asad and that she "loved" him. She wanted to know if my wife Jill, who is also a journalist, and I would serve as his sponsors for an IFY year at Brookhouse, which would mean covering one-third of his tuition and taking on a kind of mentorship role. Asad and I had already begun work on this book, and privately I worried that becoming too involved in his life would complicate writing about him. I would be violating what I considered one of the first rules of journalism: never make yourself part of the story. And yet, there hardly seemed like an alternative. What was I going to do, decline to sponsor Asad so that I could write about him? What sound code of ethics could justify that decision? Certainly no code of ethics I wanted to live by.

And so my interviews with Asad became interspersed with study sessions and trips to buy books and school uniforms. Some weekends, he studied for the SAT at our house, posting up silently at the dining room table while Jill and I worked in the living room. It had been close to fifteen years since I took the SAT. But on the day Asad bought his copy of *The Official SAT Study Guide*, I sat with him for several hours trying to give him a general overview of the exam. At length, we turned to one of the reading comprehension sections and worked through the questions together. The section consisted of two short passages on an obscure scientific topic—cell biology, I think. The questions asked us to compare and contrast the passages, and to make some inferences. When we had finished, we flipped to the annotated answer key at the back of the book— and discovered that nearly all of our answers were wrong. I did my best to explain why we had erred, but my reasoning must have sounded shaky, because after he had let me ramble for a minute or two, Asad turned to me and smiled. "That's okay," he said in a gentle, gracious tone. "By now I'm pretty good at reading the instructions and just teaching myself."

. . .

Once Asad started at Brookhouse, we saw him every few weeks. Either he would come and see us on the weekend or I would visit him on campus. One day in early December, we met at the school's Wangari Maathai Sixth Form Centre, which is named for Kenya's most famous environmentalist and the first African woman to win the Nobel Prize. Asad's economics class met in one of the center's wood-paneled classrooms, whose tall, pitched windows look out on tidy garden boxes and well-tended lawns. On the walls were dozens of bulletin boards, many of them smothered in felt pennants and other promotional materials from U.S., Canadian, and British colleges: Oberlin, Tufts, and Swarthmore flags formed a colorful radial on one board. Flyers tacked to another urged students to

visit Vanderbilt and William and Mary. A brochure for Columbia University boasted of "one of the most diverse and talented
student bodies in the world."

Other boards were covered in photos of Brookhouse pupils engaged in various student activities: sports, theater, study
abroad in Europe and Asia. One labeled "Servant Leadership"
showed student volunteers helping to build classrooms and
dorms at what looked like a rural Kenyan school. The rudimentary structures were dark and cramped, but they resembled
many of the schools I had seen in poorer parts of the country:
single-story concrete buildings topped with corrugated metal
roofs. "Imagine being squeezed into such a small space," read
the caption above one photo, which showed two dozen or so
Brookhouse volunteers crammed behind a few wooden desks.
"Notice the poor floor, missing window panes, and not enough
furniture." Another photo showed a young boy in a blue uniform, presumably a student at the school, smiling with his
hands clasped together in appreciation: "THANK YOU," the
caption read.

Asad and I paused for a moment in front of the board. It
occurred to me that the school in the photos, which evidently
struck whomever had written the captions as impossibly poor,
was probably better resourced than Abdul Aziz Primary, and
similar to Daraja Mbili, the high school Asad had attended in
Kisii. Asad looked at the photos and then at me and rolled his
eyes. "Here they are helping the poor," he said archly. "And

here the poor are saying, 'Thank you.'" One of the first observations Asad had shared with me about his new classmates was that they seemed to relish their position of privilege relative to other Kenyans. That a vast underclass was doomed to live in desperate slums only heightened these students' feelings of self-worth and sense of entitlement. "This is what I'm talking about—they enjoy the contrast," he said now.

Later, he took me through the boarding students' quarters, past an oversize chessboard set in the middle of a grassy quad, and down a series of red-brick pathways bounded by carefully trimmed hedges. All around us, students in russet crested blazers hurried this way and that, looking purposeful and self-assured. I wondered how it all must look through Asad's eyes. I knew he was cynical about the rich and powerful—it was one of my favorite things about him. But I wondered if the experience of being here would change him, either by kindling resentment within him or—worse, I thought—by causing him to grow cynical about the entire enterprise of education. I didn't doubt that attending Brookhouse had been the right decision. A single year here could open more doors for Asad than a lifetime of self-directed study. But I worried that it might come at a cost: his love for learning.

We stopped briefly at the dining hall, with its gleaming, freshly mopped floors and humming soda machines. "This is where I've had some of my biggest scandals," Asad said with a laugh, explaining that his unfamiliarity with cutlery had initially provoked snickers, and that he had once been told off by a teacher for forgetting to wear shoes. So much was still brand-new to him that he seemed to be experiencing a kind of sensory overload.

But if the etiquette faux pas were easily shrugged off, he seemed much more worried about another scandal in which he had become embroiled—the one caused by his lack of a passport. Asad had told me about Mrs. Chaudry, and about how she had reacted when he finally got up the courage to tell her he was a refugee. The issue had since been resolved, but he was still convinced she was upset with him. No matter what he did, she seemed to regard him with disdain. "In this world, everyone assumes the poor to be bad," he said. "They just assume you're going to destroy the place."

Months later, after Asad had been admitted to Princeton, I asked Mrs. Chaudry about her initial opposition to letting Asad into Brookhouse. It was the middle of the school day and she had just come from the cafeteria, where she had had to reprimand two boys caught disrupting an exam. "You see, I'm always the bad guy," she said, looking harried and distracted as she motioned for me to sit. Mrs. Chaudry has long straight hair, full cheeks, and dark, owlish eyes that betrayed a lack of sleep. Contrary to what Mr. Mulindi had told me about the contentious decision to admit Asad, she said she hadn't known about his special circumstances, and she certainly hadn't opposed letting him in. "Initially, I didn't know he was a refugee. He didn't open up. I just knew he's a scholarship student," she said, adding that she regretted having badgered him about the passport. She explained that she had been under pressure to register all the students, and that she hadn't realized that he might feel singled out. "I felt bad later on, when I found out everything," she said.

As if to say what she really thought of Asad, Mrs. Chaudry handed me the letter of recommendation she had sent to Cardiff and Bristol universities on his behalf. It showed A's as his predicted grades in all four subjects, and reported that he was a student with "high academic abilities and a pedantic approach to learning" who will "strive hard to realize his ambition." In closing, she had written, "I highly recommend him to join your institution."

...

The decision to apply to American colleges as well as British ones was Asad's. But it was informed in part by a conversation I had with Ajay around the time he and Antonia decided to grant Asad a Beacon Scholarship. In explaining the terms of the scholarship, Ajay had been at pains to emphasize that his program wouldn't automatically support Asad's college education, even if he was admitted to one of the Beacon partner universities. He would need to apply again, and there would be even stiffer competition at the university level. As a result,

Ajay told me, it was important for Asad to have a backup plan in case he was unsuccessful. I said I understood, and that Asad was also considering applying to some American colleges.

In retrospect, it was clear that Ajay didn't intend for the backup plan to compete with the Beacon Scholarship. Later, he would tell me that he had expected Asad to apply to American colleges only after the Beacon had made its decision one way or the other. Ajay saw each Beacon Scholarship as a long-term investment, and he wanted the recipient to remain in the program long enough to reap the rewards. "We look at probabilities," Ajay told me. "Once we say, 'All right, we're going to invest in you,' then we want to see that likelihood, that probability of that vision being fulfilled with this child or young person." He added, "We're in for the long run, we are a long-term player. We look at getting [each scholar] educated and then we work toward transitioning them into the workplace, and then keeping in touch with them."

These expectations hadn't been clear to me from the outset, and to the extent that I had a say in the decision, I was driven by two main concerns. The first was helping Asad leave Kenya as quickly as possible, since I worried that his undocumented status put him in danger. The second was cost. Covering one-third of Asad's tuition and boarding fee at Brookhouse had been one thing, but I wasn't at all sure that my wife and I would be able to cover the same for a British university: $10,000–$15,000 a year for three to four years would be a lot on two journalists' salaries. Admission to a top U.S. university was a long shot, but it would likely come with a scholarship that would make it financially feasible for us. Regrettably, I didn't think to communicate all this to Ajay, and Asad's decision to pursue both opportunities simultaneously would set in motion his unfortunate and sudden rupture with Ajay and the Beacon Scholarship.

...

During the months that Asad was preparing his applications, he often seemed overwhelmed. He was juggling his studies, his SAT prep, and caring for his younger siblings. There was a new crisis almost every day, it seemed. And often, Jill and I would only learn about these crises *after* they had been resolved.

A few weeks after he had returned from Somalia, and a week or two before he started at Brookhouse, Asad had written about his journey through al-Shabab territory in an article in the *New York Times*. The article appeared under the headline "My Parents' Country, in the Grip of the Shabab," and it detailed many of the harsh tactics employed by the militant group. It was a portrait of a world few people had seen, and the BBC's Somali service translated part of the article and read it aloud on the air. Soon Eastleigh was buzzing with rumors about the real identity of the daring Somali journalist who went by the pen name Asad Hussein.

Eastleigh is a vibrant but hardscrabble place, full of brash street vendors and wobbly rickshaws and bustling garment shops. It is not as dangerous as some other Nairobi neighborhoods, despite what many Kenyans believe. But its mosques have incubated violent ideologies, and a small but significant minority of its residents sympathize with al-Shabab. The rest live with the knowledge that the group's shadowy network of spies, known as the Amniyat, has eyes and ears everywhere.

Asad had received threatening phone calls and text messages before. His story in *Sahan* about Halima, the tea lady who had been forced into an arranged marriage and then abandoned, had ignited outrage among conservative Somalis who thought it was too critical of Islam. Even his article about Fatuma Omar Ismail, the engineering student who won the WUSC, had angered some in Dadaab who opposed women's education after someone at the UN reprinted and distributed it in the camp, perhaps thinking it would inspire others. But now he had his younger siblings to worry about, and the renewed barrage of threats unnerved him. Sometimes, he could hear only breathing on the other end of the line. Other times, a voice would say he was being watched or that his days were numbered.

Asad didn't tell me about the threats until later. In fact, I only found out about them because he eventually decided to move his siblings out of Eastleigh. He had started at Brookhouse by then and needed me to write to the boarding master, a man named Graham Omasire, to request permission for him to leave campus for the weekend. He planned to move his siblings across town to a working-class neighborhood near the airport, where there were fewer Somalis and presumably fewer al-Shabab spies.

But there would be other dangers in the new neighborhood unrelated to terrorism. Abdi Malik and Habiba would have a harder time blending in, and they would need to worry more about the police. Sure enough, not long after the move, Asad needed permission to leave campus again—this time to bail his younger brother out of jail. Abdi Malik had been stopped on the street and, unable to produce a *kitambulisho*, hauled to the station and threatened with deportation. By now Asad was expert at handling these situations, and he managed to extract his brother for the equivalent of $10. Still, each time he dealt with the Kenyan government, I worried it would end badly.

The cascade of Asad-related crises became a kind of drumbeat to our lives: Brookhouse, the College Board, the Kenyan government, and UNHCR all threatened to upend his best-laid plans at various times. Gradually, Asad began to evince a kind of gallows humor. New obstacles would present themselves almost daily, necessitating unplanned and invariably inconvenient solutions. One battle at a time, I would tell him. "You know, Colonel Buendía fought thirty-two wars," he said once over dinner after a particularly exasperating day, referring to the second son of José Arcadio Buendía, the founding patriarch of Macondo. "But then he died very suddenly."

For much of the year, UNHCR was auditing the rolls of registered refugees, and Asad worried he would have to race back to Dadaab to be counted. If he lost his refugee status, he would have no recognized identity at all, and no way to apply for a travel document if he was accepted to university abroad. So much was out of his hands that I found myself repeating the same refrain again and again: All you can do is your best, and everything else will come down to luck. Looking back, I'm embarrassed this old chestnut was the best that I could do. Both of us knew that luck was the hidden subtext of nearly every aspect of our lives. It explained the massive wealth and opportunity deficit between us, why I could fly to New York or Paris or Sydney on a whim and he couldn't legally leave the camp where he had been born. Both of us also knew something else: that disguising luck as worth or achievement was how those deficits were maintained.

But luck seemed in short supply that spring, as the rejection letters trickled in. Later Asad would let me in on the creeping despair he felt during this period, but at the time I could tell he was doing his best to seem strong. Still, even I felt the weight of the rejections piling up. "Only the Ivies and Stanford are left," he wrote to me after receiving bad news from Bowdoin. "And unless fate opens up its arms, there's little chance there will be good news."

On the night Asad was due to hear from Princeton and

Harvard, I was in Washington, D.C., for work. It was cold and rainy, and I had forgotten to pack an umbrella. Waiting out a temporary deluge under the awning of an apartment building on Rhode Island Avenue, I opened the Twitter app on my phone. It was the middle of the night in Kenya, and I wasn't expecting to hear from Asad until the next day. So I was surprised to see a direct message from him: "Rejected from all. Accepted to Princeton. I am crying," it read. Below he had sent a screenshot of the acceptance letter, with the bright orange Tiger logo at the top. *Could it really be true?* I thought, suddenly feeling as if I had been hit by a tidal wave.

I dialed Asad's number at once, but I was unable to get through. Maybe it was the rain or maybe it was just the shoddy cell service in parts of Nairobi, but the call kept cutting out. Finally, on the fourth or fifth try, we managed to connect. On the other end of the line, though, all I could hear were sobs.

· · ·

Three months later we were on our way to Princeton. Jill and I had flown with Asad from Nairobi to New York, not wanting to miss his arrival in the United States. By chance, we arrived at JFK on the Fourth of July; Asad had been invited to enroll in a summer program for incoming freshmen who were the first in their families to attend college. We planned to drop him off on campus, but first we wanted to show him New York, the city where Jill had lived for fifteen years before we moved to Kenya. Maryan had flown in from Richland to surprise her brother. It would be the first time they had seen each other in more than six years.

The taxi dropped us in the Brooklyn neighborhood of Crown Heights, at the apartment of a friend who had generously offered to put us up for the holiday weekend. The place was on one of those picturesque blocks of prewar brownstones, with wide welcoming stoops that ascend to grand double doors. We were on the sidewalk, still groggy from more than twenty-four hours of travel and sweating in the heat, when Maryan's taxi pulled up. It took a moment for Asad to register the slender figure who alighted on the curb, her head and shoulders wrapped in a delicate pink and purple scarf. But then it clicked, and his arms and legs went slack. She raced to him and scooped him up in her arms, supporting the weight of his limp body as they embraced for what seemed like several minutes, tears streaming down both of their cheeks. I tried to imagine what must be going through their minds. But even after so many hours of listening to them recount their stories, I realized I had no idea. There was simply no way for me to fully comprehend what they had endured—or the depth of the strength that had brought them both through it.

For the rest of the day, Asad kept protesting that we had "ambushed" him with Maryan's visit. But for all his complaining, he seemed happier than I'd ever seen him. We had breakfast at a Mexican restaurant, where he announced that horchata was his "favorite American food so far." Later that evening, the four of us watched the fireworks together from the Williamsburg waterfront. In a photo Jill took that night, Maryan and Asad are leaning into each other, a distant but contented look in both of their eyes, as Maryan takes a selfie. Behind them across the East River is the Manhattan skyline. Above them, a single firework lights up the sky.

XII

PRINCETON

Princeton, New Jersey, Fall 2018

The Firestone Library looms over Princeton University like a great Gothic cathedral. Named for the tire magnate who pillaged West Africa for rubber, it contains seventy miles of bookshelves and more than 7 million volumes. (Until the Guangzhou Library in southern China opened in 2013, Firestone was the largest open-stack library in the world.) Inside its dimly lit bowels, you can wander for hours without passing through the same corridor twice. Row after row of crowded shelves seem to extend forever, a labyrinth of aging hardbacks suffused with the quiet hum of fluorescent lights.

"There are books on everything you can imagine," Asad exclaimed one afternoon as he led me through the stacks. Jill and I had helped him move into his dorm, and for the rest of the summer and fall he and I had touched base every week or so. During breaks, he alternated between visiting his parents and sister in Richland and staying with us in Washington, D.C., where we had moved into a small Federal townhouse near Howard University. And every few months, I rented a car from the Enterprise on Georgia Avenue and drove the three and a half hours up I-95 to visit him. "History, philosophy, medicine—there are books written in languages you will never be able to read. I never knew something like this existed," he said, jabbing a lanky arm toward a row of thick reference texts. It was outlandish to think he had ever dreamed of reading every book in the world, he added with a laugh. "You're standing here surrounded by these books, and that's when you feel how insignificant you are."

During his first months on campus, he spent hours at a time underground in the stacks. There were books he had read at Abdul Aziz Primary that he hadn't been able to track down anywhere since. He was amazed to find them all at Firestone, usually first editions that had been shelved the year they were published. It was a way to gradually orient himself, locating artifacts from his past in this place that felt so foreign. One of the first books he went in search of was *The House of Hunger* by the Zimbabwean novelist Dambudzo Marechera. Born to a poor family in what was then apartheid Rhodesia, Marechera had gone to study at Oxford University in England, but struggled with culture shock and mental illness before ultimately getting expelled. His collection of semi-autobiographical short stories, published in 1978, had been a favorite of Asad's back in his Room 101 days; Marechera himself had fascinated him, being one of a very few prominent African writers who didn't hail from the middle class. "He calls the place he grew up 'House of Hunger,'" Asad told me. "And Dadaab in many ways was a house of hunger, too."

Asad also sought out books by people who had gone to Princeton or been affiliated with the university. He wanted to know what Michelle Obama and Jeff Bezos had thought about when they were students here, so he checked out their senior theses. "I couldn't grasp much of that one," he said of Bezos's thesis, which was on computer science and electrical engineering. But Michelle Obama's, titled "Princeton-educated Blacks and the Black Community," resonated deeply with him. "My experiences at Princeton have made me far more aware of my 'Blackness' than ever before," the future First Lady had written. It was an experience Asad would have in his own way, coming from a place where ethnicity and religion had been the dominant cleavages, not race. Whereas in Kenya he had been a Somali and a refugee, at Princeton he was suddenly an African, and a black man on a campus that was still very much the domain of whites. "I was a foreigner in Kenya too, but I shared the culture," he recalled. "Being a refugee and being illegal removed me one level. But when I came here, I was twice removed from the society, and I had to figure out the customs and the culture."

One thing that struck him right away was that most people at Princeton had a backstory that bound them to the American project in some way. They were Asian Americans or African Americans, Irish Americans or Pakistani Americans. But what was he? "That's part of the agony of statelessness," he explained. There were also the classmates who were just American—no modifier needed. Many of them were second- and third-generation Princetonians. They exuded a rarified quality that he couldn't quite place, as if they had sprung straight from the mythological American firmament—boat shoes, pastel button-downs, and all.

It was these students who seemed to embody the customs and the culture of Princeton most fully, and it was these students who seemed to work the hardest to forestall change. In one of the strangest annual traditions Asad encountered, hundreds of hopeful sophomores attempted to "bicker" their way into exclusive "eating clubs" housed in the imposing brick-and-stone mansions on Prospect Avenue. Woodrow Wilson had tried to get rid of the eating clubs back in 1906, when he was president of the university. Fourteen years later, F. Scott Fitzgerald would describe the most famous of them, Ivy Club, as "detached and breathlessly aristocratic." Seventy years after that, Ivy would admit its first woman—by court order. And it wasn't just the bickering sophomores that seemed stuck in the past. Toward the end of his first semester, Asad got a job manning the library checkout desk as part of his work-study program. One day, an older gentleman strode up to the desk looking agitated. One of the cabinets on the third floor was locked, the man complained, adding that it used to be kept open when he was a student.

"When was that?" Asad inquired.

"Nineteen seventy-two," the man replied.

There were other things that seemed strangely antiquated about his new home. Whenever Harvard or Yale came up, whether because Princeton was due to face off against one of them in football or basketball or because some important piece of research had been conducted by one of their faculty members, his classmates would boo loudly. "What is this tribalism?" he remembered thinking. "Why must we hate Harvard and Yale in order to love Princeton? This is the mentality that destroyed Somalia—so why am I being taught it at the best university in the world?"

But on a campus filled with so many extraordinary things, it was easy to brush these misgivings aside. He attended lectures by leading scholars, wrote his first article for the *Daily Princetonian*, and joined the university press club. One day he texted me a selfie with Tracy K. Smith, the poet laureate of the United States. She taught creative writing at Princeton, and Asad had dropped in for her office hours.

Each day brought new marvels that he could have scarcely imagined a year ago. He took a class in Mandarin and another that involved computer coding. He made friends from Russia and Mexico and Kentucky. He visited Six Flags and rode the highest roller coaster in the world. Despite the frenetic pace of his new life, however, he could never quite move fast enough to escape the one he had left behind. There were little things—a text from Bekar, a flyer for an Eid celebration—that would suddenly transport him back. Walking alone in the dark, he was sometimes seized with an uncontrollable feeling of dread. "I still carry the terrorism of the Kenyan police. You never fully escape it," he told me once as we trudged across campus at dusk. It was late autumn and the fallen leaves crunched loudly under our feet, the yellow bulbs of the street lamps giving the stone buildings around us a medieval glow. "You are always from Dadaab. And in Kenya, it is a crime, being from there."

There was also the guilt that weighed him down like an invisible anchor: the guilt of having escaped the misery of Dadaab when so many others had not, and the guilt of having it better at Princeton than his friends and siblings did back in Kenya. One thing Asad had noticed about other refugees from Dadaab was that many of them never looked back once they arrived in America. True, they often sent money, but their minds and their hearts seemed to want desperately to be free of that place. Those who were lucky found jobs and a rung up toward the middle class. Few sought to maintain links to their impoverished past. But Asad felt pulled in the opposite direction, his attachment to his birthplace strengthened rather than diminished by the newfound distance. Someday, he told me time and again, he would return and fight for those who remained in the camp.

One day in the middle of his second semester, Kenya renewed its threat to close Dadaab and to "expedite relocation of refugees and asylum seekers residing therein," according to a leaked official communiqué. As with previous threats, this one sent fear coursing through the camp, and through the wider Somali diaspora. For the first time in his life, Asad wasn't at the mercy of the Kenyan government. But from the safety of his dorm room, he felt a new kind of powerlessness. Now that he was in the United States, it seemed there must be something he could do to forestall this injustice—or at least to make others feel the way he did. He fired off an email to the editor at the *New York Times* who had published his article from Somalia. "Only way to contain my anger," he wrote to me afterward.

But Asad's F-1 student visa forbade any form of employment aside from his work-study program. If Immigration and Customs Enforcement became aware of an op-ed for which he received payment, he could be deported. When I read his message, I felt a sudden jolt of panic and excused myself from a meeting to beg him not to put his future at risk. It was a gray and unseasonably cold day in Washington, D.C., and out the second-floor window of my office I watched as tightly bundled figures outside struggled against the wind. The phone rang several times before Asad picked up. "Heyyyy, Ty," he said as always. But his voice sounded thin and a little uneven, as if he hadn't slept in days. I made my case as cheerily as I could, pointing out that there would be plenty of time to write op-eds after graduation—or after he had applied for asylum, should he decide to do so. But the longer I babbled, the more I felt like a coward. Cautious, self-interested decisions like the one I was counseling surely helped to explain the continued existence of places like Dadaab. I wanted Asad to be brave and speak out— just not too brave, and not yet. I also wanted this conversation to be over, I suddenly realized, and for us to both forget it ever happened. There was an uncomfortable silence, and then a quiet, exasperated reply. "I guess I'm still trapped after all," he said, trailing off. "The never-ending saga of Asad."

...

"I'm trapped by my [refugee] status. And in fact, I don't see any opportunity."

Bekar's expression was grave, almost sullen. He wore black wing tips, navy slacks, and a shiny maroon blazer embroidered with what looked like oak leaves. Around him on the floor of the one-bedroom flat he shared with two Kenyan Somalis, both students like him, was a clutter of shoes and bags and crumpled blue exam booklets. Three narrow beds were wedged against the walls, piled high with laundry and other collegiate detritus. Above them the ceiling was a swirl of water damage, peeling in parts and adorned with a single naked bulb. To save money, the landlord cut the power during the day, but as evening fell the light flickered to life.

It was February 2019, and I had returned to Kenya to track down some of Asad's childhood friends. Earlier in the day, Bekar had met me at the bus station in Eldoret, the highland town in western Kenya where he was studying for a degree in public health. We had walked to Moi University's College of Health Sciences, set amid tall trees and dark green hedges, where he had spent the last two years acquiring skills and knowledge he might never be legally allowed to use. Ever practical, he told me he had chosen public health because it offered the best chance of leading to work in Kenya's burgeoning NGO sector. Or if not there, then in local government. His classes were in hands-on subjects: sanitation and human waste management. He had initially thought he might find work as a community health officer. "But there's no way," he said now. "You need a national ID."

There were few options for a student in Bekar's position. The Albert Einstein German Academic Refugee Initiative paid his tuition and gave him a small stipend every semester. He was allowed to move freely around the country during the period of his studies. But after graduation, he would be on his own again, educated but no more qualified to work in the eyes of the Kenyan government. There were ways to acquire a *kitambulisho*, shady off-the-books ways that other refugees he knew had tried. But such methods were expensive—the bribes ran hundreds if not thousands of dollars—and there was no guarantee they would work. Sometimes corrupt government officials simply walked off with your money. As a refugee with no status, there was nothing you could do about it.

The alternative was unlivable, though. The only jobs in the camps were the so-called "incentive" jobs, the eternal apprenticeships that paid $80 a month and held out no hope for advancement. Bekar had already worked one of these dead-end jobs, at an organization called Refugee Education Trust. He had been the camp coordinator's assistant in Ifo 2, and briefly, the "acting" camp coordinator for main Ifo. The promotion had come with additional responsibilities but no additional pay. Once, he had raced to gather survey data for an international donor on a tight deadline, only to have his Kenyan colleagues take credit for his work. "You do everything in that hot sun. They take the data to the donor, and it's like they have done it," he recalled. "But, in fact, we are the ones who have done it."

Bekar said he couldn't bear the thought of going back to that. He asked if I knew of any graduate programs in the United States that might give him a scholarship like the one Asad had received. There was a look of quiet desperation chiseled on his face, his eyes darkly expectant. Night had fallen now and outside the cicadas were sawing laboriously from the trees. I hesitated for a moment. I didn't know much about public health programs in particular, but I knew that graduate scholarships for foreign students tended to be extremely competitive. I said as much, but offered to help him research programs anyway.

Later, he followed up with me over WhatsApp:

"everythin is possible if u work hard"

"hard work pays"

"I will consider any degree program."

. . .

My phone buzzed on the nightstand in our bedroom in Washington, D.C., revealing a series of texts from Asad. "This is not the America I imagined," the first message read. Next came a screengrab from the local news outlet *Planet Princeton:* "White Supremacist Group Set to March in Princeton on Saturday," the headline blared.

Since Asad had arrived in the United States, scarcely a week had gone by without a new cruel and senseless immigration policy or a hate crime against a minority group. The president, who as a candidate inveighed against Mexican "rapists" and later saw "very fine people on both sides" of a deadly white supremacist rally in Charlottesville, seemed to have unleashed something powerful and noxious on our politics—or else revealed it to have been simmering not far from the surface all along. Swastikas were turning up on elementary schools. Children were breaking down in class, afraid of suddenly being deported or separated from their parents. Once a beacon of hope, America was becoming a nation of fear.

Asad had felt the shift long before he arrived in the United States. The travel ban had affected him personally, and the public perception of America had changed markedly in his final months in Kenya. On one of his last nights in Nairobi, his friends had thrown him a going-away party. "Congrats, and be safe, Asad," they had written in red frosting on a cake they bought for the occasion. "Don't get shot" one friend had added, scribbling on the cardboard cake box. "Dodge the bullets!" joked another. Still, after a lifetime of dreaming about the United States, he hadn't expected to find it riven with discord and consumed by hate.

By the time he arrived at Princeton, the language of the alt-right had crept into the national discourse on immigration. For much of the preceding year, Fox News and Breitbart, among other conservative outlets, had carried breathless coverage of the so-called "migrant caravans" wending their way up from Central America. To Asad, the national debate felt like a referendum on his personhood. Here he was struggling with his own identity as a refugee and an immigrant, and the whole country was suddenly having the same discussion on a national scale. "You begin to ask yourself, 'Who am I?' You question yourself—an identity crisis in your life," he confided. "And that is bolstered by the conversation about immigrants, and seeing your identity as an immigrant in a new country. Your identity is the subject of a national conversation, but you're still trying to figure out things for yourself. Everyone is now talking about that, which is really strange."

In his second semester, Asad took a class in the journalism department on writing about the refugee and immigrant experience. The small seminar of a dozen or so students met in the historic Joseph Henry House, a yellow Federal-style house with dark shutters on the northern edge of campus. Asad was one of only three black students in the class, and the only refugee, and he soon found that the conversation often centered on him. His classmates all meant well, but he disliked when they walked on eggshells around him, or worse, when they seemed to feel sorry for him. "Some people would pity you, which I hate," he recalled. "I almost became the focus of that class, because I was living the subject of the class. I felt beneficial to the other students, but for me it was a constant struggle."

In the spring, the professor took the students to observe real immigration court proceedings in New York City. Asad sat in on the asylum hearing of a family from Central America. When he described the experience after the fact, he couldn't recall many of the details, it was so visceral to him. "This family is fighting for their life. And then the system just makes a judgment. It's so fast. Like that," he said, waving his hand to indicate an assembly line–like progression. In this case, the judgment was a positive one, and the family received asylum. Asad remembered watching the mother break down in tears of relief, but feeling strangely detached, as if he were floating on a separate plane of existence. The idea that his own family might one day be reunited in a country that had accepted all of them seemed as distant and improbable as ever.

XIII

GOOBE

Dadaab, Kenya, May 2019

Early morning light streaked across the parched scrublands of eastern Kenya as the stocky, snub-nosed DASH 8-100 began a labored descent toward the only sliver of asphalt for miles. From my seat at the window, I watched as the dry, inhospitable landscape slid by below, a patchwork of orange and dark green that gradually took shape as sand and desert acacias. Then, as if out of nowhere, the wilderness ended and row after row of miniature dwellings appeared. Tiny flecks of white and silver, arranged in precise rectangular grids, they stretched to the horizon like diodes on a dusty circuit board. As we descended farther and the scene shed some of its unreality, I had the feeling that I had just covered a vast distance, that I was entering a world separated from the hustle and bustle of Nairobi by more than the 300 miles I had just traveled.

Across the aisle from me in the opposite window, Maryan recorded our approach to Dadaab on her iPhone. She wore a gray sweater and a silky purple dress, her hair swaddled tightly in a bright yellow hijab. Since we had arrived in Nairobi, she had seemed in a daze, disoriented, perhaps, by the dramatic change the city had undergone in the fourteen years she had been in the United States. The previous day, we had returned to Eastleigh to try to find the secret apartment she had lived in when she first left Dadaab. It was nearing the end of Ramadan, and throngs of women in colorful abayas were surging in and out of shops, stocking up on clothes and gifts and sweets. "None of this was here before," Maryan had said as we passed a new Arab-inspired shopping center. "Everything is new." We finally located her old building near the intersection of First Avenue and Ninth Street. It was a quaint two-story bungalow with royal blue trim, and it was surrounded by towering new high-rises that made it look comically out of place. The only other building she had recognized on the entire street was a low-slung storefront with a few boarded-up kiosks stacked out front. Spray-painted above the door in red letters: "THIS PLOT IS NOT FOR SALE. Beware of conmen!!"

The idea of a joint trip to Kenya had been hers. Not long after Asad had arrived in the United States, Maryan and her family had moved across the country to Milwaukee so that Sharif and Kaltuma could be close to other Somalis they had known from Dadaab. They had rented a two-bedroom apartment in Castle Manor, a neglected slice of suburbia not far from the airport. The building was dark, with no-frills appliances and shag carpets that smelled faintly of cigarettes and cleaning fluid. In the winter, snow piled up on the roof, and long icicles dripped down from the eaves. The bitter Wisconsin cold came as a shock to Sharif and Kaltuma, singeing their lungs and leaving their faces numb. Kaltuma got a salaried job for the first time in her life, making sandwiches at a food company called Sandwich Bros. of Wisconsin. Sharif mostly refused to leave the house during the coldest months, unless it was to go to the mosque.

The daily stresses that had defined Maryan's life while she waited for her parents' green cards had receded somewhat but not disappeared. She still owed thousands of dollars to friends and credit card companies, and scarcely a week went by without some new financial mishap that set her back further. One day, Kaltuma suddenly fell ill and had to be hospitalized overnight. The bill came to $5,399.92—or more than two months of after-tax wages at the Amazon warehouse where Maryan had started working the night shift. A few months later, a letter arrived from the United States District Court for the Eastern District of Washington. "Subpoena to Testify at a Hearing or Trial in a Criminal Case," the subject line read. Years before, it turned out, the clerk at the corner store in Richland, Washington, where Maryan used to buy groceries, had been caught exchanging food stamps for cash—a federal crime about which

Maryan was now being summoned to testify. Never mind that she had a job and five kids to look after or two elderly parents who spoke next to no English. "You are commanded to appear in the United States district court at the time, date, and place shown below to testify in this criminal case," the letter read in part.

Maryan had been juggling these and many other daily hardships when I had gone to visit her and her parents in Milwaukee, but she had spent hours patiently recounting her story, and helping me make sense of old documents, emails, and medical records. I played video games with her youngest son as she rummaged through her closet for immigration forms I wanted to see, and picked up her older kids (and half a dozen neighbors) from Quranic school in her gray Honda Odyssey while she searched for still more records from her parents' green card applications. The more we delved into the past, the more driven she seemed to find an answer to the one question that had haunted her for all these years: Why had her family been left behind in Dadaab when seemingly every other Ashraf family had been resettled? She had her suspicions, of course, based on what had happened to Ayaan in Goobe's office. But she wanted a definitive answer—hard proof that there had been foul play and that her family's case wasn't just a tragic accident. "What *happened* to us?" she asked over and over. "I just want to know the truth."

I wasn't at all sure we would be able to find the kind of

conclusive answer she sought. There were so many reasons a resettlement case could be derailed, legitimately or illegitimately, and so many bottlenecks in which corrupt or malevolent officials could create artificial delays. Delays also tended to compound each other, as the individuals who shared cases fell out of sync, their refugee mandates and medical clearances expiring at different times and preventing everyone from moving forward. Getting sick or having a child could set you back, as could falling victim to various scams or extortion schemes. There were dozens if not hundreds of officials who had a hand in shepherding each individual case through a complicated interagency process that involved UNHCR, the International Organization for Migration (IOM), and various U.S. agencies and contractors. Any one of them could have been the cause, or *a cause,* of her family's misfortune.

Around the time we began discussing a trip to Dadaab to look for answers, the Irish journalist Sally Hayden published a damning exposé of corruption in the UN resettlement process, focusing on Kenya and four other countries with significant refugee populations. In Dadaab, Hayden had uncovered a bribery ring that included a UNHCR resettlement officer who had collected tens of thousands of dollars to advance certain cases and to swap new identities into others that were already cleared for visas. Cases that were in the final stages of vetting were being sold for thousands of dollars, leaving refugees who had been specially selected because of their vulnerability stranded for years. It was "the perfect petri dish of corruption," one UNHCR staffer had told Hayden.

Without the family's medical records from IOM, it would be difficult to prove that Goobe had deliberately sabotaged their case, either because Ayaan had rebuffed his advances or because he had been angling for a bribe. When Asad had taken Sharif for his final medical checkup at IOM's Nairobi office in late 2016—the only time he had been examined outside of Dadaab—the nurse had only been able to find records dating back a few years. Close to a decade's worth of medical records appeared to have vanished—a fact that would be highly suspicious if we could establish conclusively that it was true. But when Sharif made an official request for the records through a doctor in the United States, IOM officials in Nairobi refused to turn them over, citing a blanket policy against sharing them with former patients. Even if we had managed to get them, I wondered if they could be trusted. According to Hayden's reporting, UNHCR officials had tampered with case records in order to cover their tracks.

But there was another way to approach a question like this. If an IOM medical official had attempted to prey on at least one refugee under his care, perhaps there were other victims or witnesses who would be willing to talk. They could help us understand how Goobe had abused his office, if indeed he had, and whether he would have been in a position to derail a resettlement case without raising any red flags from within the organization. It wasn't the exact question Maryan had in mind, but it was close enough that we both wanted to see if we could find an answer. From a journalistic perspective, there were plenty of commonsense reasons not to bring an aggrieved party like Maryan into what was meant to be an objective inquiry. But she had worked as a professional translator, including on sensitive legal matters, and I knew she wanted the truth as much as I did. She had spent a third of her life wondering whether this man had ripped apart her family. This was her investigation. (It was Asad's as well, but without a passport or permanent legal status in the United States, we decided it was too risky for him to join us.)

The plane landed with a thud and taxied to the end of the runway. In the black pleather seats around us were aid workers of various stripes, many of them wearing vests emblazoned with the logos of their organizations: UNHCR, Mercy Corps, Kenya Red Cross, among others. They were Kenyans mostly, along with a few white faces. Aside from Maryan, I don't think there was another Somali on the plane. We filed out into the clear morning light, squinting as we made our way toward a herd of idling 4x4s with massive tusklike antennas. Maryan and I climbed into a gray Toyota Hilux I had rented, and after picking up a pair of armed escorts from the police station, we sped off towards Ifo.

• • •

It was winter in Kenya, and Dadaab was greener than the last time I had been there. Short trees had sprouted up between the colossal termite mounds that residents jokingly refer to as mountains, fighting admirably against the shifting desert sands. From the airstrip, it is almost five miles to Ifo, along rough unpaved roads that constantly merge and subdivide. The Land Cruisers and pickup trucks that speed back and forth along them churn up huge clouds of dust that follow them like contrails. Troops of scrawny kids occasionally wave and call out to them, then turn to shield their eyes.

We had decided to begin our search in Ifo because that's where Maryan's family had lived. There were still a few Ashraf families living there, some who had arrived after the initial resettlement wave in 2004 and some, it turned out, who had been left behind as well. Our plan was to find out whether there were other families who had been through the medical checkups year after year, and to ask them if they had experienced anything unusual. Having to repeat the exams multiple times wasn't necessarily proof of anything, since IOM physicals expire after a year and must be renewed if other aspects of a refugee's case are still pending. But those who had been to the medical center again and again would have had the greatest chance of coming into contact with Goobe, we reasoned. Perhaps they had seen something.

It turned out to be harder than we had imagined. People welcomed us into their homes, and though it was Ramadan and most of them were fasting, offered us water and a place to sit in the shade. Almost everyone knew someone who had been through the medical exams more than once. Friends led us to friends, neighbors to neighbors. There were far more people stranded in a similar situation than I had expected to find, people who had received "conditional approval" letters from U.S. Citizenship and Immigration Services as far back as 2009, but whose cases had stalled out in the final stages. But most people grew sullen or nervous when we asked about IOM and the medical exams. Women tsked impatiently, and men shook their heads and looked at the ground. "You will never get the truth," said one woman who had endured eight physicals. "Sometimes we are scared to say anything, because it can come back and haunt us," said another, a young mother who had been waiting to be resettled since 2009. "If you say anything, they can just cancel your case and you will stay here forever."

Ifo is like a maze, a dense warren of family compounds, each ringed by identical thorn scrub hedges that knit together into continuous barriers. The effect is to make the roads feel like tunnels, twisting passageways that confound the uninitiated while at the same time failing to shield people's personal lives from public view. Nothing is private when you live five or eight to a room and your wall backs up against your neighbor's, when you can peer through a tangle of brambles into his or her living room. In lieu of individual secrets, there seemed to be communal secrets, and after a while, the communal secrets started tumbling out.

"He will ask, 'Are you married? Are you dating? Are you

talking to anyone?'" one woman said of Goobe. She had approached us nervously at the home of another family, after hearing that we were asking about IOM. She was slightly built, with delicate features and wide hazel eyes. She told us that Goobe had propositioned her during a physical exam in 2008. When she refused, her case suddenly stopped moving forward. "Some people will accept to be violated so they can leave. Some people won't accept and they are stuck," she said.

Maryan and I agreed to withhold the woman's name, along with the names of other women who came forward after her to tell their stories. Most were terrified of retribution, either in the form of further delays to their resettlement cases or in the form of violence. Some said they had been threatened by IOM medical staff if they complained to anyone. From what these women told us, there were two ways to ensure you passed your physical exam: money or sex. "Everything is money, money, money or yourself," said one woman who went through her first medical exam in 2016 and whose case has been pending since then. "If you want to be on tomorrow's flight, then I have to sleep with you tonight," was how another woman summed up the unspoken rule of IOM's medical center in Dadaab.

Altogether, more than a dozen refugees told us separately that they had experienced either unwanted sexual advances or the solicitation of a bribe from a member of IOM's medical staff. Maryan and I conducted the interviews in the presence of a second translator I had hired, lest there be any question about her objectivity. We were also careful not to prejudice any of our subjects by asking leading questions. We asked the women only if they had experienced anything unusual at IOM, and if so, with whom. In interview after interview, three names came up as the nexus of alleged corruption dating back to the mid-2000s, when the Ashraf resettlement began: Abdirahman Mohamed, who was the head nurse until around 2008; Goobe, whose real name is Alibashir Mohamed and who worked inter-mittently as an IOM nurse in Dadaab between 2004 and 2008, when he replaced Abdirahman as the head nurse; and an op-erations assistant named Abdulahi Musa, also known as Bisle, or "Straight Hair," who was hired by IOM around 2007 and according to many of the women was the most brazen of the lot. Abdirahman and Bisle had since left IOM—Abdirahman married a refugee and went to the United States sometime around 2008, where he is now rumored to be living under an-other name, and Bisle was quietly let go in early 2018. But at the time we arrived in Dadaab, Goobe was still the head nurse at IOM.

Multiple women accused all three men of attempting to exploit them sexually. Bisle was often tasked with calling the refugees in from the waiting area, and three different women said that he propositioned them while they walked together to the examination room. When the women refused, he threat-ened to torpedo their resettlement prospects. "I can cancel your case. Don't you know that?" he told one woman in 2008.

She had been through six physicals prior to that, but gave up and stopped reporting for medical exams after her run-in with Bisle. Abdirahman and Goobe tended to be subtler, using suggestive come-ons to feel out the receptiveness of their quarry. "Why don't you help me help you?" and "I hope we can understand each other" were the kinds of phrases a single mother who had recently undergone a C-section remembered Abdirahman saying. When she refused to disrobe in his office, he threw her out angrily, saying, "You will see if your case goes forward." That was in 2007 or 2008, she thinks, and her case is still pending.

The accusations against Goobe followed a similar pattern. An interpreter who had worked as a contractor for the IOM medical staff in Dadaab beginning in 2004 said that in 2008 Goobe pushed her to sleep with him in exchange for more regular work. "If you accept, then you have a job. If not, then he's not going to call you," she said. She refused and the work dried up. In the time they worked together, she said she saw both Goobe and Abdirahman pressuring younger refugee women to have sex with them, particularly unmarried women. "If they see a pretty girl in a case, they will ask, 'Can I marry you?' And that's not allowed," the interpreter said.

In addition to sex, all three men allegedly sought bribes. Male and female refugees we spoke to reported being asked to "give me something" in exchange for medical clearance. A common code word for bribe was "soda"—a word that had popped up in Hayden's reporting on corruption at UNHCR. Often, the three IOM medical staffers appeared to have used intermediaries, incentive workers drawn from the refugee population who would show up at people's homes offering to advance their cases in exchange for money. Multiple refugees also said they had paid bribes directly to all three men. One refugee who had been through eight medical exams as well as three additional tuberculosis screenings said both Bisle and Abdirahman had asked him for money in 2007: "They asked me for a lot of money, but all I had was one thousand shillings," he said. According to the interpreter, the going rate was between $500 and $3,000—or 50,000 and 300,000 shillings—far above what most refugees could afford to pay.

Maryan and I had gathered a significant body of evidence from refugees, including the interpreter, who said they had been victimized by all three men. We had conducted the interviews independently and in different parts of the camp, so we could be sure that none of the women had coordinated their stories. We had also cross-referenced the dates of the alleged incidents with what we knew about the three men's employment history. All of it checked out. The only thing we didn't know for certain was whether the medical staff had actually followed through on their threats to cause unnecessary delays to refugees' resettlement cases. That changed when we tracked down a former IOM staffer who had worked in Dadaab during the initial Ashraf resettlement phase in the mid-2000s.

The staffer, who asked to remain anonymous because he still works with UN agencies in Kenya, described how Abdirahman and Goobe both called refugees in for unnecessary procedures in order to extract bribes or sexual favors. One ruse the former staffer had observed directly involved calling refugees back for second or third physicals long before their first one had expired. Another involved spurious tuberculosis screenings. Mandatory chest X-rays taken in Dadaab would be sent to Nairobi for evaluation, after which a list of patients with abnormalities would be sent back for additional diagnostic procedures, including sputum smears and cultures. Abdirahman and Goobe would add additional names to the list of patients being called in for follow-ups. These patients' X-rays had come back clear, but the nurses would nonetheless ask them to come in for sputum collection, which often required a full day of waiting or more. According to the former IOM staffer, it was an open secret that these inconveniences would disappear for a fee. If the refugees didn't know the jig before they arrived, they would quickly learn about it—either from other refugees or from the nurses themselves.

This description matched up perfectly with the testimony of one male refugee who had spoken to us earlier in the week. The man had been for seven physicals beginning in 2009, and each time he had been called back for sputum cultures, even though the results of the previous tests had always come back negative. Goobe never asked him for a bribe directly, he said, but someone he didn't know visited his house and suggested that he pay "something" in order to resolve his medical issue. "They are messing us up because they want something," he said. "People who can afford it will take one or two medical exams and then they will go to the U.S.A. If you can't afford, you will just stay."

After four days of interviews, my notebooks were over-flowing with damning testimony, and the list of victims kept on growing. It seemed impossible that such brazen misconduct could have gone unchecked for so many years at an agency whose purpose was to protect the vulnerable. But in nearly a decade as a foreign correspondent and editor, I had never been a part of an investigation that was this clear-cut. None of the women had been willing to put their names on the record. But given the intense climate of fear, and the very real threat of retaliation, I hadn't expected them to. Thousands of miles from Dadaab in mainly Western cities, the #MeToo movement was exposing not just a litany of misdeeds by powerful men but the hidden forces that had protected them for years. At the apex of newsrooms and production companies, among other venerable perches, these men had used money, influence, and sometimes teams of lawyers and shadowy operatives to cover their tracks. In Dadaab, the power differentials were even bigger, and there was no one to turn to for help. With the power to halt or ad-vance resettlement cases, IOM officials quite literally held the refugees' lives in their hands.

The independent Office of the Inspector General for IOM would eventually open an official investigation as a result of the testimony Maryan and I gathered. And Leonard Doyle, a spokesperson for IOM in Geneva, would confirm that one of the alleged predators, Bisle, had previously been investigated by the Inspector General's office as a result of anonymous claims of fraudulent extortion. But the office had been unable to verify the claims against him, and it had eventually closed the investigation. Bisle's contract with IOM expired in January 2018, and IOM elected not to renew it "due to a downsizing of IOM Kenya operations," according to Doyle.

IOM claimed to have no information about Abdirahman, and I was never able to track him down under his new name in the United States. Both Goobe and Bisle denied the allegations against them, but Goobe acknowledged that he too had been previously investigated by IOM after a family of refugees accused him of corruption (although Doyle claimed to have no record of that investigation). "There was one allegation that came to the office. It was investigated and disqualified. . . . They wanted to scapegoat using my name," Goobe told me when I reached him by phone. He said he was "shocked" to hear of the new allegations and strongly denied having sought bribes or sex from anyone under his care or supervision. "That's against my professional ethics, my faith, my everything," he said.

At the time the manuscript for this book was finalized,

Doyle said that IOM's inspectors had "not yet uncovered sufficient evidence to substantiate the allegations" against the organization's staff members but that the investigation was still ongoing. In the nearly six months since Maryan and I had first presented IOM with our findings, inspectors had visited Minnesota, Wisconsin, and South Dakota to interview refugees who had been resettled from Dadaab. For reasons IOM did not divulge, however, its inspectors had not yet visited the refugee camp itself—where all of the women Maryan and I interviewed still live. Meanwhile, Goobe remained on the job.

. . .

The main operations hub for IOM, UNHCR, and various other aid agencies in Dadaab is inside a massive rectangular compound near the airstrip. More than a mile and a half in circumference, the complex is ringed by multiple layers of fencing, the outermost built to withstand a bomb blast and topped by a triple coil of razor wire. On the day Maryan and I had arrived, several desperate refugee families had been camped in front of the entrance to protest food ration cuts. They were unable to get inside to speak with anyone, but unwilling to go home. With the families blocking the gate, we waited in the truck for a few minutes while our driver conferred with the guards, who were contracted through a private security company called G4S. When our driver returned, he said we had been directed to use a second entrance roughly a quarter of a mile on down the road. He added that he had overheard one of the guards speaking with someone from UNHCR on his shortwave radio: "Get the journalists out of there before they make a story about the protesters," the UNHCR staffer had said. "And sort those refugees out so they are not there when the journalists leave."

Because the camp is regarded as insecure—several kidnappings over the years had given rise to the government's policy of providing journalists with armed escorts—we had arranged to stay inside UNHCR's fortified compound. It was a delicate arrangement to say the least, investigating one UN agency as guests of another. But it was an awkward dance I had done many times before as a journalist working in places like Dadaab, where commercial airlines don't fly or where there are few safe places to stay outside of a UN base. In order to maintain my independence, my rule of thumb had always been to pay my own way; never accept a free flight or lodging, even if UN officials offered them. We had followed my rule on this trip as well, covering the costs of our flight and hiring two rooms in UNHCR's guesthouse at a rate of $40 per night.

Once inside the blast-proof walls, one understands at once why the refugees are kept at a safe distance. A lush oasis of neem trees and delicate bougainvillea, the world inhabited by UN employees exists in jarring contrast to the world they are there to serve. Staff members can play tennis in the evenings and sip cold Tusker lagers at a thatched gazebo bar, which turns into a club on weekend nights. While reduced food rations in the camp mean that most refugees survive on a little more than half of the UN's own recommended daily caloric intake, those living on the compound can choose from at least two separate dining areas, or belong to a private dining club. "I knew there was a different world behind these walls, but I didn't know it was like this," Maryan said one evening over plates heaped with rice, cabbage and beef stew. We sat at a thick wooden table in a spacious tiled courtyard, a blue parasol flapping gently above our heads.

I asked if it felt strange to finally be inside this place after so many years of being shut out. It was a dumb question, and I immediately regretted asking it. What I really meant was did she feel angry knowing that this existed in such close proximity to so much suffering. "You know, this place is supposed to be for refugees," she said, as if she understood what I had been trying to say. "They are supposed to hear our voices, but they can't hear our voices over their walls." After a long silence, she added, "This place is so powerful. It can destroy you, and there is nothing you can do."

• • •

Two days before Maryan and I arrived in Dadaab, a student named Mohamed Abdulrahman Ahmed hanged himself from a narrow support beam in his home. He was twenty-six years old and in the middle of repeating his final year of high school in Ifo. "His dream was to go to Canada and help his family," Faisal Gedi, the director of the school he attended, told me.

Mohamed had been a star student for most of high school, scoring consistently high marks all the way up. He had been elected class monitor, the highest student office, so many years in a row that his classmates called him Qaddafi—not because of any character defect but because he had been their leader long enough to be a Middle Eastern despot.

Mohamed reportedly left a suicide note in which he said he had fallen short of his aspirations. The year before, he had scored a D+ on the national high school exam, far below his expectations and nowhere close to qualifying for the WUSC. His parents had already given up on life in Dadaab, and returned to Somalia through the UN's voluntary repatriation program. He had stayed behind to finish high school, living alone and dedicating nearly every waking hour to his studies. The principal, a bald middle-aged man named Elias Ndonga, said Mohamed often reported to school as early as 5:30 a.m. and didn't leave until late in the evening. Ndonga had resorted to barring him from campus after hours so that he would go home.

In his short adult life, Mohamed had watched the world turn its back on Dadaab. Not only was Kenya periodically threatening to close the camp, but the UN had slashed food rations by 30 percent, a move that registered with many refugees as an attempt to starve them out. Then came the Trump travel ban, which affected more than 14,000 people in Dadaab and all but severed the link with the United States. With so few routes remaining to a better life, the WUSC had taken on even greater importance. "It was the WUSC or it was nothing," Asad had remembered thinking when he was a student. It seemed likely that Mohamed had felt the same way.

The day before I visited Mohamed's school, I had gone to Towfiq Secondary School, where Asad had started high school a little more than eight years prior. A cluster of six rectangular classrooms made from cinderblocks and corrugated metal, it sat on a rather forlorn plot of land on the farthest margins of Ifo, partially overgrown with weeds and dusted with sand. Staked to the ground out front was a fading, handwritten sign that declared as the school's mission to "transform learners into dependable individuals in the society."

I had tried to picture fourteen-year-old Asad sitting under one of the nearby clusters of trees, hearing about the WUSC for the first time. It made me think of a conversation I had had with Maryan earlier in the trip, about how much of American culture—and in particular, the culture of American individualism—had seeped into Dadaab over the years. She had said that when she was in school here more than twenty years ago, people were less concerned with individual achievement and more concerned with lifting families and communities up. A family that was healthy and united was better than one with a child in America, even if that child could send back money. But the more removed people became from their old lives in Somalia, the more they seemed to embrace a quasi-American notion of individualism. "My whole life, it seems, I've been living the American dream," Asad had written in the essay I had edited at *Foreign Policy*. "I just don't know how much longer I can bear to live it outside of America."

How cruel it seemed, in retrospect, to have preached the gospel of individualism in a land where there was, at best, limited free will. For a time, the resettlement flights to America—rare enough to be golden tickets, common enough to feel within reach—had helped keep the faith alive. But as the departures dwindled and then dried up altogether, the promise of a better future became a source of pain instead of hope. In Kakuma Refugee Camp, which houses roughly a quarter of a million mainly South Sudanese refugees near Kenya's western border, nine refugees took their own lives in the span of sixteen months after Trump's travel ban went into effect. The spate of suicides so unnerved aid workers that they began confiscating potentially deadly objects: "Knives. Wire. Battery acid. Rat poison. Rope," the Reuters correspondent Maggie Fick reported.

The pall cast by the travel ban was inescapable in Dadaab. Everywhere Maryan and I went, people told us how they or their loved ones had given up on ever being resettled. They were either steeling themselves to spend the rest of their lives in Dadaab or weighing the possibility of going back to Somalia. "Since Trump, resettlement is over," Ndonga, the headmaster, told me. "The refugees have nowhere to go now. No resettlement. No integration. No work."

Mohamed, the boy who hanged himself, had had friends in the United States. The photos they posted on Facebook had deeply affected him, according to Ramadan Ibrahim, a business manager at the school who had known him well. "Most of the time, he talked about resettlement, about leaving the camp for a better life," he told me. "Number one was the scholarship to Canada, but he also talked about the U.S., about his friends there, about their beautiful life."

As Maryan and I left the school, she said it had never occurred to her to consider how her social media posts might affect someone who was still stranded in the camp. "You just post things online. It's your life, but you never really think about what it does to people here," she said. "Imagine a twenty-six-year-old just hanging himself because there is no hope for the future." I could tell she was thinking about her brother, about how under different circumstances that might have been him.

Later that night, I spoke with Asad on the phone. For the last week, we had corresponded nearly every day as I provided updates on the progress of our investigation. "There is something deeply powerful about you and Maryan being in Dadaab," he had written to me the day before. "I've been coming to that compound where you are staying since I was eight. . . . I heard people's complaints; that changed the way I look at life and the world. I witnessed a tragedy. What is worse, I could never talk about it."

Now we were talking about it, tearing open an old wound

that I knew must be painful for him. I hoped that our investigation would give him closure, but I knew that in some ways this was a selfish act on my part—dredging up the past so that I could write a book about it. That night on the phone, I could hear the pain in his voice. "I haven't slept since I learned of that boy's suicide," he said. He sounded distraught, almost frantic—the same way he had sounded a few months earlier, after Kenya had again threatened to close Dadaab and he had found himself powerless even to write about it without jeopardizing his student visa. Now I imagined him in his dorm room at Princeton, looking out the window on a campus freshly beautified for alumni reunions and struggling with the thought of everyone he had left behind. He had finished his final exams the week before, and was preparing to move to New York City for a summer internship with the International Rescue Committee. Soon, Princeton would be flooded with nostalgic revelers, dressed in orange and black Tiger jackets and belting out the lyrics to "Old Nassau." A place more distant from Dadaab I could scarcely fathom.

The next morning, I scrolled through Twitter, as I often do when I'm waking up. Alongside news that Mexico was cracking down on Central American immigrants at Trump's behest, and that the U.S. president had called London Mayor Sadiq Khan a "loser," I saw a tweet Asad had posted. "Dear students in Dadaab," it began. "Truth is, the world has failed us. When you are faced with the throes of life in a refugee camp, there's only so much you can do. We have been sold a lie: there's no level of personal drive or hard work that can pull you out of a refugee camp. I can confirm you are the most driven students anywhere. Even those at Princeton, supposedly the world's best college, can hardly meet your discipline and commitment." In closing, he added, "Please don't despair. Don't kill yourself. There's much the world has to learn from you."

Later that day, Maryan and I drove the short distance to the airstrip to catch our flight back to Nairobi. A dry desert wind rustled the thorny shrubs on either side of the road, blowing fine grains of sand in through the windows of our truck. I thought about the tens of thousands of people who are now Americans who spent time in this place, and about how different their lives must be in Seattle or Minneapolis or Milwaukee. At length, we passed a group of girls in long, flowing abayas. They looked young enough to be in school, but it was Eid, the final day of Ramadan, and the schools were closed. I wondered if the girls had heard about the boy who had hanged himself, and if they shared his feeling of hopelessness. I wondered if they too had spent years studying for a scholarship or waiting to begin a new life somewhere far away. And I wondered if after everything that had happened in the last two and a half years, they still dreamed of America.

XIV

A SENSE OF BELONGING

New York, July 2019

On the Fourth of July in 2019, the first anniversary of Asad's arrival in the United States, we were in the bleachers at MCU Park on Coney Island, twelve rows back from the first-base line. It was a fine night for a baseball game. Hot and humid, it was the kind of night when a pitcher can really get loose and put a little extra zip on his fastball. The diamond was aglow with stadium lights and beyond the outfield, over the thin sash of the home run fence, a tangle of roller coasters looped and dived. The Brooklyn Cyclones had trailed the Aberdeen IronBirds, a class A affiliate of the Baltimore Orioles, for most of the game. But that hardly seemed to bother the crowd of jubilant, partially inebriated fans scarfing down Nathan's Famous hot dogs. They were here to celebrate America's day of independence by observing one of its most sacred traditions. Everything else, including the score, was secondary.

Over the past year, Trump's vicious attacks on immigrants and refugees, and the glee with which his supporters cheered them, had shaken my faith in America as a force for good. More than the invasion of Iraq, which had revealed the bankruptcy of much of the establishment, and more than the never-ending war on terror, whose collateral damage I had seen up close as a foreign correspondent, the rancorous chauvinism of the Trump era seemed to hint at a deeper flaw in our national character, one that harkened back to the sins of an older age but that was unmistakably a creature of our venal, hyper-connected one. Still, I continued to believe in the American experiment, flawed as it has always been, and I hoped that Asad would look for the good as well as the bad. It was not a coincidence, I thought, that Americans had responded to the first two years of Trump's presidency by electing the youngest and most diverse Congress in U.S. history.

One of those newly elected representatives, Ilhan Omar, had once been a refugee in Kenya as well. Her story would not have been possible in that country, and I could tell that Asad was both proud of and inspired by her success. "There are not a lot of places where you can come and really be a part of it," he mused. "Run it sometimes, be in charge of the district where you live." But I could also see that the steady drumbeat of anti-immigrant stories, and open hostility of the U.S. government, was taking a toll on him. Later that summer, Trump would suggest that four minority congresswomen, including Omar, should "go back" and "help fix the totally broken and crime-infested places from which they came." Only Omar, who became a U.S. citizen nearly two decades prior when she was seventeen, had been born outside the United States.

For Asad, the fraught political climate reinforced a feeling of rootlessness. For his entire life, he had been an outsider, an exile with no clear origin or home. A simple question for most people—where are you from?—necessitated an entire conversation for him. He had hoped to find that elusive sense of belonging here in the United States. Instead, he had found a country wrestling with its own identity.

It was against this backdrop that Asad confronted the question of asylum. His student visa granted him the right to remain in the United States for five years. But after that, he would have to find an employer to sponsor him or return to Kenya, where, like Bekar, he would face travel restrictions and a bar on work. If he returned to Somalia, he would face a catalogue of disadvantages and dangers, starting with his membership in a minority clan, the Ashraf, and extending through to his critical writings about certain conservative Somali traditions and about al-Shabab. Even in Eastleigh, his article in the *New York Times* about traveling back to Somalia had put a target on his back.

But the thought of putting himself at the mercy of the U.S.

government also unnerved him. It felt like being "trapped under the sea struggling to breathe, but it is your worst enemy who is reaching down to rescue you," he told me. There was another problem: claiming asylum would require him to re-narrate his own story so that he was a victim. He had never allowed himself to go over to that "side," as he called it, to think of himself that way. "You know it's pretty depressing," he said of the asylum process. "It's basically giving all the reasons you would die if you weren't here."

Asad had spent the early months of the summer wrestling with this dilemma. He had excelled during his first year at Princeton, and won a special fellowship from the university that covered his expenses for a summer internship in New York City. He had chosen to work at the International Rescue Committee, the organization that helped resettle his sister back in 2005. As a "peer mentor" at the IRC's Refugee Youth Summer Academy, he was now helping other young refugees navigate the same confounding web of cultural differences that he had confronted a year earlier. That gave him more of a stake in America, he supposed, but it didn't make him feel any less ambivalent about being at its mercy. He sensed that many of his students were similarly affected by the unwelcoming national mood. They were from all over the world, but mainly from Central and South America. A handful hailed from West Africa; none were from Somalia. Even at a summer camp run by the IRC, Trump's travel ban was inescapable.

...

That night at the baseball stadium Asad was still undecided about seeking asylum. I hoped he would go through with the claim, mainly because I thought that it would give him the best chance to fulfill his dream of becoming a novelist. But I also thought he might still find what he was looking for in the United States. The game was part of my pitch. Easily a third of the players on both teams had been born outside the country, in Cuba, the Dominican Republic, and Venezuela, among other places. I had grown up playing baseball, and even spent a year after high school pitching for a semi-professional team in Fort Lauderdale, Florida, where I was one of a very few native English speakers on the roster. The Playball Internationals, we had been called, a name that could apply to both of the teams Asad and I had come to watch. I rambled on about the game throughout most of the night, and Asad nodded and smiled good-naturedly, despite having little understanding of the rules. At the end of nine innings, the score was tied two-two and both of us were ready for the fireworks display that had been promised after the game.

The IronBirds finally rallied in the top of the tenth, scoring four runs that the Cyclones couldn't answer in the bottom half of the inning. After the players had shaken hands and disappeared into their dugouts, Asad and I walked down onto the field with hundreds of other fans. We picked a spot in center field and sat down, leaning back with our palms pressed into the artificial turf. Soon, fireworks were streaking across the sky as Bruce Springsteen's "Born in the U.S.A." blared out of tinny speakers. Later, as we filed out of the stadium, Asad turned to me and said, "America, it's not perfect. Never has been, never will be. But to us at least, it has been very kind."

Author's Note

This book is a work of nonfiction. Between January 2017 and
February 2020, I conducted hundreds of hours of interviews
and reviewed hundreds of pages of documents, emails, and
other records to piece together this story. For the first year or
so of this project, I lived in Nairobi and was able to make regular trips to many of the locations described here, including
Eastleigh and the Brookhouse School. (From 2015 to 2018, I
was based in Kenya full-time as the Africa editor of *Foreign
Policy* magazine.) I made five trips back to Kenya in 2018 and
2019, visiting Dadaab refugee camp and Eldoret, among other
places. Additional reporting took me to Mogadishu, Milwaukee, Seattle, and Princeton.

I was present for many of the events described here, although none that occurred before January 2017. The dialogue

that appears in quotation marks was either witnessed by me or recounted to me by someone who witnessed it. Memories or thoughts attributed to individuals in quotation marks are verbatim quotes from those characters. Memories or thoughts that are italicized were paraphrased by me. All of the names are real, except for Ayaan, Idil, Divya Chaudry, and David Ongwae. I have also identified several characters by their first names only. I have used this approach on request, because disclosing a person's identity could expose them to harm, or because I was unable to reach them for comment.

In addition to interviews and primary documents, I relied on a number of published works, including articles that Asad wrote for *Foreign Policy*, *The Guardian*, the *New York Times*, the *Daily Nation*, and *Sahan*. I also drew on *The State of Africa: A History of the Continent Since Independence* by Martin Meredith; *Digital Democracy, Analogue Politics: How the Internet Era Is Transforming Kenya* by Nanjala Nyabola; *City of Thorns: Nine Lives in the World's Largest Refugee Camp* by Ben Rawlence; *Africa's First Democrats: Somalia's Aden A. Osman and Abdirazak H. Hussen* by Abdi Ismail Samatar; *Clan Cleansing in Somalia: The Ruinous Legacy of 1991* by Lidwien Kapteijns; *Al-Shabaab in Somalia: The History and Ideology of a Militant Islamist Group 2005–2012* by Stig Jarle Hansen; and *Getting Somalia Wrong?: Faith, War and Hope in a Shattered State* by Mary Harper. I am indebted to Kevin Sieff of the *Washington Post* for his reporting on the WUSC scholarship and to

Sally Hayden for her investigative work for NBC. In addition, I have drawn on news items from *The Guardian*, *Wired*, Reuters, the *New York Times*, *Foreign Policy*, the *Daily Nation*, *The Standard*, and *The Star*, as well as reports published by the Brookings Institution, the Center for Strategic and International Studies, Oxfam, CARE, and Human Rights Watch.

Acknowledgments

I am grateful to all of the people who agreed to be interviewed for this book, especially Asad, Maryan, and Bekar, who shared so much of themselves. You inspire me. Dr. Sue and Mr. Mulindi, thanks for always making time for me, and for taking a chance on Asad.

I am also indebted to my literary agent, Gail Ross, without whom this book never would have seen the light of day. You gave it to me straight when I pitched you the first, flawed version of this project, and you helped me craft it into the book it is today. Michael Flamini, my editor at St. Martin's Press, supported, encouraged, and occasionally saved me from myself. Thanks also to Tom Shroder and Rebecca Frankel, whose incisive edits improved the manuscript; to Nanjala Nyabola, Hassan Ghedi Santur, Alexis Okeowo, Nichole Sobecki,

Kevin Sieff, Tristan McConnell, and the late Richard Todd, all of whom provided invaluable feedback on early chapters or drafts; and to Julie Schwietert Collazo, who meticulously fact-checked this book. Others who offered help, advice, and companionship during long months of writing, or who went out of their way to support Asad in his mission to get a college education, are Mark Jia, Habin Chung, Rob Lalka, Sam Kleiner, Fagan Harris, Simon Boehme, James Sprankle, Zelalem Mulat, Shravan Vidyarthi, Liz Vidyarthi, Jisas Lemasagarai, Celine Clery, Cyril Villemain, Max Bearak, Matina Stevis, Mike Onyiego, Maeve Francis, Abigail Higgins, Neha Wadekar, Samir Ibrahim, Lauren Bohn, James Smith, Sarah Cramer Smith, Greg Presto, Sara Melillo, Jackson Maina, Daniel Knowles, Tom Stackpole, Davis Rosborough, Geoff Curfman, Shannon Browne, Julie Rubenstein, Sara Robinson, Anne Dana, Diane Lucas, Kate Goldwater, Maryclaire Grace, Priscilla Camacho, Jeffrey Toobin, Martha Lyman, and Dan Berger. Special thanks to my brother Colten; to Jennifer Davis; to my in-laws, Michael Filipovic and Mary Filipovic; and to the entire Allison and Lohrer clans.

Thanks also to my colleagues at *Foreign Affairs* for your advice and encouragement. I am particularly grateful to Dan Kurtz-Phelan and Laura Secor—both of you helped to advance this project. Ben Pauker, if you hadn't signed off on that first assignment in Dadaab for *Foreign Policy,* I never would have met Asad. You took me under your wing at FP, and gave me the latitude to do much of the reporting that laid the groundwork for this book. Susan Glasser, Blake Hounshell, Peter Scoblic, Joshua Keating, Cameron Abadi, David Kenner, and Colum Lynch, you taught me most of what I know about journalism. Thanks also to Frank Henry, Peter Nilsson, Joel Thomas-Adams, Bernie Baker, Elyce Perico, Celia Riahi, Heather Ferguson, Ramzi Salti, Jack Rakove, Adeel Malik, Timofey Agarin, and Trina Vargo for sharing your wisdom and for encouraging me to write.

Mom and Dad, you both read more iterations of this manuscript than anyone else, including my editors. Thank you for your loving support, and for catching all those typos! And finally, Jill, I owe the greatest debt to you. Thank you for nurturing and supporting this project as if it were your own, for carrying me when I was too exhausted to carry myself, and for reading and rereading dozens of iterations of this book. It would not exist without you.

ABOUT THE AUTHOR

Ty McCormick is an editor at *Foreign Affairs*, the magazine published by the Council on Foreign Relations in New York. A former foreign correspondent in Nairobi and before that in Cairo, he has reported from more than a dozen countries in Africa and the Middle East. He has written for *The New York Times*, the *Los Angeles Times*, *The Washington Post*, *Newsweek*, *The New Republic*, and *National Geographic*, among others. From 2015 to 2018, he served as Africa editor of *Foreign Policy*, where he led a team of reporters who won a Robert F. Kennedy Journalism Award for a series on African migration. He is a graduate of Stanford, Oxford, and the Queen's University Belfast, where he was a Mitchell Scholar.